Run for Fun

To Cheryl:

Hope you will enjoy my
odyssey, starting in Latvia,
surviving W.W.II camps in
Germany and coming to
America (Yea !??)

Pete Petersons

Run for Fun

A Memoir

Atis V. Petersons

DEDICATION

To all of the former runners who enjoyed being part of our Run for Fun community and who contributed so much to making it possible.

To the Latvians who were scattered throughout the world but now live in freedom.

To my wife, Joyce, and my loving daughters, Marni and Corey, who provided motivation for me to write my memoir. When I became discouraged, they inspired me to complete the task.

CONTENTS

THE LATVIAN MARTYR
(FREEDOM FIGHTER)

Mr. Atis, better known as Mr. Pete of Pete's Palace

"Pete's Palace"

A FARM IN LATVIA

My life began in 1934 on our family farm near the town of Rūjiena, in northern Latvia. Our village, Naukšēni, was about ten miles from the Estonian border. Throughout my childhood, I have heard it said that my mother only stopped working in the fields long enough to give birth to me. Two of our female apprentices prepared a tub of hot water and acted as midwives. I was the youngest of three children, joining my five-year-old brother, Modris, and two-year-old sister, Jausma. My thirty-two-year-old father, Voldemars, and twenty-nine-year-old mother, Vera, dedicated their lives to our family and our beautiful and productive piece of land.

Growing up in a natural environment allowed me to enjoy my younger days in total freedom and harmony. I was a curious boy who always stayed active, I couldn't stand still! Whenever neighbors or visitors came to our farm, they usually found me on the run, watching me hurrying from our barn to the winding river, or from the windmill to the birch tree groves. Running was as natural for me as breathing air. Having so many intriguing places on our farm, I could run in any direction, go as far as I wanted. I would love to sprint downhill in the rain, feeling the cold air as raindrops hit my face. This is how I discovered new sights with my dog Rex beside me.

The following passage in Guy De Maupassant's memoir sums up how our family felt about our farm: "I became attached to it by deep roots, the profound and delicate roots which attach a man to the soil on which his ancestors were born and died, to the traditions, their usages, their food, the local expressions, the peculiar language of its neighbors, the smell of the soil, the neighbors around you, and the atmosphere itself."

Our beloved farm represented freedom. The groves of ancient oaks surrounding our land served as guardians of the fields and meadows. I spent hours wandering through the woods, trying to learn its secrets. The woods were my refuge; I felt that the trees were a roof between the sky and me. I wandered through the densest parts, picking mushrooms and tasting wild berries. The quiet sounds of the forest were often interrupted by a flock of wild geese flying overhead, as they approached the small lake near our home. They became frequent guests who always returned. Hearing their trumpet sounds and seeing them gliding on the lake's glassy surface also added to my rich childhood memoires. I could explore and wander with a purpose or simply relax. Whatever I chose, I was never bored.

Unlike the giant monoculture agribusiness farms of today, ours was a paradise of diversity. We raised everything we needed to thrive as a family and as a commercial enterprise in our community. We grew wheat, sugar beets, potatoes, and orchard fruits. We raised dairy cows, chickens, pigs, and goats. We had horses to pull the plows and wagons, and we grew hay to feed the horses. The manure from all the animals went back into the fields as fertilizer for the next season's crops. Nothing was wasted. We had no electricity yet, so we had to store our foodstuffs in a cold storage in the basement. It remained cool during most of the year, but we still had to continuously replenish our meats and items that could spoil easily. Our smokehouse was a blessing since it kept some of the meats safe. Still to this day, Latvians in exile love to smoke their own salmon and other fish. We also built a sauna house, common in the Nordic countries.

1.The Petersons family with two farm workers.
My dog Rex shown on bottom right, 1940.

The happiest moments of my childhood were spent on our farm. Modris, Jausma, and I loved to gather eggs and pick strawberries. We jumped from our two-story barn into a pile of hay. When I was six, my parents brought home a shaggy brown shepherd dog named Rex. Rex always had a happy disposition, and we soon were inseparable. He followed me whenever I ran through the woods or along the streams, and he helped when it was my turn to herd the cows from barn to pasture and back.

Living on a farm was an adventure for one's senses. I will never forget the taste of my mother's freshly baked bread and homemade butter. I loved watching her use a long wooden paddle to pull the steaming loaves from a kiln that my father had built. It was often served with honey from our own hives and warm milk that had just been hauled into the house from the barn. Although our special oven would be a perfect place to bake pizzas today, we used it to make *pīrāgs*, a Latvian specialty made from chopped egg, bacon, and onions, all wrapped inside fresh dough and baked to a golden brown. For desserts, we had rhubarb and apple pies usually served with homemade ice cream.

A family farm such as ours required dedicated and resourceful caretakers, which accurately describes my parents. I have few memories of them idle. My father was strongly built with broad shoulders. He was not afraid of hard work; no task was too demanding. He believed God blessed him with a temperament and constitution for the physical and mental challenges that were part of everyday life on a farm. He, along with two hired apprentices, rebuilt the house and barns and maintained all the farm equipment. He continued to seek education in advanced forms of agriculture, especially animal husbandry and dairy production. By the time we left our farm, it had won awards for being the most productive in our county. In order to supplement our farm income, my father also worked at a local creamery. My father and mother modeled a work ethic that has endured and guided my siblings and me throughout our lives. Whereas my father showed his love through the pride of providing a home and food for his family, my mother was more demonstrative, patient, and forgiving. When my father was called to work at the creamery, my mother quietly became the soul of our farm. We appreciated her love of nature and living creatures. Whenever she found a knife on the table with the sharp edge facing straight up, she used the incident to demonstrate how little things can be important. She reminded us that "an angel's wing may be cut." To this day, I never leave a knife with the blade facing up, and I use her words to reinforce the learning process with my own children. She also reminded us "to finish the plate if you want the sun to shine tomorrow." These were all simple but powerful memories of a loving mother. Her gentle nature did not, however, prevent her from hard work. She never shied away from the arduous physical work that was necessary to keep a farm running. One day, when she noticed that our bull was agitated and aggressive, she calmly directed us to move to a safe part of the corral. Once we were secure behind a fence, we watched her approach the animal and talk to it until it quieted down. Our mother was the only person who was able to restrain him effectively. She was also the only member of our family who was brave enough to gather honey. She patiently put her hands into the hive while hundreds of bees surrounded her masked face. She was seldom stung.

Atis in mother's lap - Modris - Jausma in father's lap

2. The Petersons family on the farm. From left; Jausma,
Vera, Atis, Voldemars and Modris, 1942.

of the farms and surrounding countryside. The neighboring farm-houses looked like matchboxes. Making sure our parents were not watching, we often jumped into haystacks from the second-story barn window. Our father let us use his potato basket for a basketball goal. We cut the bottom out, attached it to the barn, and tested our basket-shooting skills with an old soccer ball. With so much room around the farm and so many different places to explore, life was never dull.

Our school was about five kilometers from our farm. During my first years, my parents dropped me off with a supply of food, and I stayed at the school for the rest of the week. During my last years at the school, my parents let me walk or run by myself. I usually ran, hoping that I would be able to avoid the neighbors' dogs. Despite my running, I would still attract dogs, which loved to chase anything that moved. In those cases, I would slow to a walk until the dogs lost interest and then resume running after they returned to their house. Years later, while running a mile race for Lincoln High School in Seattle, a dog broke loose and nipped me a number of times, forcing me to slow down until the chase ended. I lost the race, but it brought back fond memories of my walks to school in Latvia.

3. Playing on the farm windmill.
From bottom; Modris, Jausma and Atis, 1943.

CHANGE OF SEASONS IN LATVIA

The seasons were distinct in Latvia, each bringing its own joys and opportunities. I live in Southern California now, which has beautiful weather throughout the year. Even so, I still miss the beautiful spring and fall colors that I enjoyed during my childhood on the farm. The warm summers enabled us to enjoy outdoor activities throughout the day. June was the most exciting month of the summer because of the many traditional festivities. The highlight activity was Jani, the midsummer-night festival of June 23. It took place throughout the country when summer was at its peak and farmers were anticipating the busy harvest season.

The celebrations and rituals were a tribute to all of the spirits of the home, field, and forest. They were intended to bring forth a bountiful harvest and healthy livestock. Preparations started weeks ahead. Beer had to be brewed, homemade cheese processed, and for us younger kids, it meant weeding gardens, raking the porch, and cleaning the yard. The day before the celebration was the best day to gather medicinal herbs and flowers for wreaths. Flowers were believed to bring luck and wealth and are still one of the most important symbols of Latvian festivities. I remember being surrounded by roses of every color. Men's wreaths were made of oak leaves, whereas women wore flower chaplets. Animals were not forgotten: they were adorned with birch-tree branches. I remember Jani as a night of singing, dancing, and wonderful food. We brought prepared dishes, especially homemade cheese and beer, along with the traditional pīrāgs. With over nine hundred folk songs, Latvia is known as one of the Baltic "singing nations." Everyone knew the songs, and our neighbors enthusiastically formed impromptu choruses to sing their favorites. The most famous song, "Ligo, Ligo!" ("Cheer, Cheer!"), was sung repeatedly throughout the day and night. Groups of revelers from other villages joined us, singing songs while building bonfires. I enjoyed watching as a wooden barrel filled with firewood was hoisted atop a tall pole. The barrel was lit, and the torch could be seen from great distances. The nonstop revelry made it difficult for anyone to sleep.

Like other cultural expressions, Latvian music is one of the best ways to chronicle the history of our country. A remarkable collection of folklore (fairytales, riddles, proverbs, and especially folk songs) has been passed from generation to generation by word of mouth. It has survived and thrived to this day. The largest folk festival was held in the capital city of Riga, attracting up to forty thousand singers dressed in costumes representing every area of Latvia. Even today, Latvians hold song festivals in larger cities throughout the world.

The conclusion of summer always came too soon. We were never ready for the cool nights, morning fog, or the rapidly changing skies. Our parents worried about getting the harvesting done in time. Fortunately, our neighbors helped each other with the wheat and hay harvests. I loved watching elders thrash the stalks of wheat with the wooden batons that were attached by ropes to long handles. We kids gathered alfalfa and rolled it into bundles. We were always in a hurry to finish the haying before the first rains. Everyone helped to transport the bundles of hay and alfalfa to the barn. There were so many neighbors involved in the process that my mother had a difficult time providing enough food for the work party. Without their help we would have never gotten the harvest completed in time. I enjoy looking at my photos of our neighbors helping with the harvest—they depict outmoded methods but also show that the cooperation of so many people could overcome the absence of modern technology.

As dark clouds raced across the sky, we saw large flocks of geese flying south. We knew winter was almost upon us. The storks, residents on our chimneys during the warmer months, gathered their young and took flight as well. The rain came almost daily and kept us indoors. Our pastures were turned into large, shallow lakes, so we had few places for our outdoor games. We looked forward to the day when the rain would turn to snow. It was freezing, but at least it gave us opportunities to go outside and enjoy winter sports. I remember getting up early, eagerly waiting for snowflakes to cover the windows and the sight of the countryside painted white. The snow would last for four months, and we enjoyed a variety of games and sports. My father built a toboggan for sledding down our small hills, and improvised ice skates for skating on the frozen lake behind our house. We sometimes dared to test our skates on a wide spot on our frozen river. There were memorable walks through our woods after a heavy snowfall. White powder blew off the downward-bending branches into our faces. It was nature's way to keep the branches from collapsing under the weight of the snow. We rolled in the snow and tossed snowballs at each other for hours, until we were finally exhausted. I remember collapsing in front of our fireplace and soaking up the warmth. We considered ourselves fortunate to live in a place with so many opportunities for outdoor recreation.

Spring awakened us to new sights and sounds. The forest burst forth with new energy, the symphony of songbirds accompanied by the rhythmic tapping of rain on newly emerged leaves. The last patches of snow melted as thunder rumbled in the distance. The heavy spring rains created a network of small streams. The new leaves on the birch trees were especially vibrant and could be seen shimmering in the spring breezes. The blossoming apple trees produced the unique fragrance of nature in the process of renewal, as if waking from a long sleep. Soon, I would need to resume my job of leading our cows to pasture, so that they, too, could savor the bounty of the season. Even Rex, after being cooped up all winter, began to bark at anything that moved.

After experiencing my childhood in such an idyllic setting, I find much in Beethoven's Sixth Symphony, *Pastoral Symphony*, that I can relate to. The piece expresses his love for nature and his ability to find equilibrium in a simple walk through the countryside. "The symphony awakens my feelings, from the trickle of a creek, the sound of birdsong, the rustle of the leaves, hearing country folk dances, the coming storm with thunder and lightning, all ending in a peaceful, tranquil atmosphere" (Beethoven). Beethoven's feelings mirror those of Guy de Maupassant's in *The Horla*, where he observes, "Everything that surrounds us, everything that we see without looking at it, everything that we touch without knowing it, everything that we handle without feeling it, everything that we meet without clearly distinguishing it, has a rapid, surprising, and inexplicable effect upon us and through them on our ideas and our being itself."

Gathering wheat for harvest

4. Harvest time on the farm, 1939.

SOVIET AND GERMAN
OCCUPATION (1940–44)

The history of Latvia is one of continuous invasion and subjuga-
tion by various conquerors. "For century after century, the im-
position of a new set of values upon the old—defeat, and then
collaboration, followed by assimilation," is how Laiks, the Latvian
newspaper in the United States, described the fate of our country.
Our lives were shattered by invasions of Soviet Russian troops, first
in 1940 and again in 1944, when they pushed out the Germans.
Having two warring "giants" on both sides of Latvia would eventually spell doom. Small nations such as Belgium, Netherlands, and
Poland also became battlefields for the invading powers. And once
again, as you read my story, it will become clear that the Baltic
countries (Latvia, Lithuania, and Estonia) faced the same fate that
Ukraine recently suffered with the Russian annexation of Crimea. If
you are a small nation and have tyrants as neighbors, God help you,
because nobody else will. The Germans considered the Poles to
be Slavs, a label synonymous with "beneath contempt." Germany's
policy of racial purification resulted in the near extermination of the
Baltic Jews. The Europeans ignored the Nazi threat by appeasing

Hitler. Winston Churchill described Europe's plan to deal with Hitler as "each one hopes that if he feeds the crocodile enough, the crocodile will eat them last." All of Europe's countries hoped that the storm would pass before their turn came to be devoured.

As bad as the Germans turned out to be, nothing matched the brutal occupation by the Russians in 1940. Latvian leaders had their throats cut and eyes gouged out. To make sure the populace remained in a state of terror, they displayed the bodies of slain leaders for all to see. Our leaders were detained, interrogated, tortured, and shot. The Germans had made tyranny into a science. We were also betrayed by our own countrymen, who aided the Communist takeover by informing on Latvian leaders. We can accept that every society has its opportunists—misfits, idealists, criminals, the disillusioned and disappointed who want to "even the score," but these collaborators had no conscience. Thousands of prominent Latvians were exiled to Siberia, and many public personalities disappeared without a trace. If a prisoner had the misfortune of being sent to one of the Siberian gulags, he had a slim chance of surviving.

Here is a snapshot from an eyewitness account of how Riga changed after the Soviet takeover, from *The Three Occupiers of Latvia—1940* produced by the Latvian Ministry of Foreign Affairs.

"Once the Soviets seized all power in late 1940, a resident in Riga observed that there was an all-too-noticeable and pervasive gloom in the reaction of Riga's population. Within days store windows were emptied and the cleanliness for which Riga was known disappeared in a whirlwind of piled trash because nobody swept the streets. Lights were turned off and owners emptied their stores. People no longer wore colorful Latvian clothing, instead choosing the drabbest attire so as to not be identified as western Bourgeoisie. Flying the national flag was forbidden, and the use of terms such as "sir" or "madam" was discouraged. Sunday was abolished as a day of rest, replaced by a day off every sixth day. Former national holidays were forbidden, and celebrating Christmas was discouraged. The defilement of their once-beautiful city disgusted the residents. Public intoxication and rudeness became commonplace, while the dignified tranquility of Riga's boulevards was replaced by the clanking of tanks. Aircraft roared overhead, and speakers continuously blared the Internationale.

Long lines for scarce goods became a feature of Latvian urban life."

We were terrified that my father could face deportation. He had been in the military and was considered to be a community leader because of his nationally recognized expertise in dairy farming. Luckily, he received warnings from neighbors and friends that he was on one of the infamous Communist lists. The Soviets were afraid that he had influence over the locals and would need to be "dealt with." Our father knew he had to hide, so we searched for a safe place in the woods where he could remain undetected. We dreaded hearing the Russian trucks pull up to our house. Our mother made sure Modris, Jausma, and I hid in the house when the troops arrived. We looked on in horror as soldiers fixed bayonets onto their rifles. They spread out and searched the house, the two barns, and any other place that looked suspicious. When they approached the haystacks behind the barn, the soldiers thrust their bayonets into the stacks. Each night we went into the woods in order to bring food to my father. The Russians stayed in our area for about a month looking for Latvians they suspected of being with the resistance. We were in constant fear that one of our neighbors or a farmworker might report our father to the Soviets, but it never happened.

When we returned to school in the fall, we discovered that Communist-indoctrinated Latvians had replaced our regular teachers.

My parents were incensed that our school was no longer Latvian, but Communist, with new teachers, books, and policies. Daily indoctrination rallies were held in the gymnasium. We were forced to march in circles while singing Communist songs that had been translated into Latvian. I don't remember any of the words (it was all Communist propaganda), but the music was the same as the Internationale, the communist national anthem. One day, as a prank, one of the boys took out the slingshot that he had hidden in his back pocket, loaded it with a rock, and broke the glass frame that contained Stalin's picture. We stood in dead silence as the picture fell down, the glass shattering on the gym floor. The boy was quickly escorted out by two Russian soldiers, and we never saw him again. When we told our father about the incident, he never let us return to the school.

THE GERMAN OCCUPATION OF LATVIA DURING WORLD WAR II

We knew the Germans were approaching Latvia from the west. Many Latvians viewed the Germans as liberators. They knew that the Germans would pass through the Baltic States on their way to Leningrad, and we didn't fear them as much as the Russians. Latvia had been part of the Hanseatic League, and we were somewhat familiar with German language and culture. The Germans were not inclined to punish Latvians unless they were known to be Russian collaborators. Our biggest fear was for draftable aged Latvians. The Germans conscripted them to fight on the Eastern Front.

In July 1941, the Germans advanced eastward and drove the Soviets out of Latvia. German authority was established, and the elimination of Jewish and Roma Latvians began. Latvian collaborators were involved in the elimination of twenty-six thousand Jews. By the end of 1941, almost all of the Jews were exterminated. Two hundred thousand Latvians were conscripted into the German army.

During the German occupation, my father met an officer who was assigned to command the troops in our area. When he visited our farm, he wanted to exchange his worn horses for our fresh ones, which we agreed to. My parents also offered the officer surplus food from our farm. We never felt threatened by the Germans because, after becoming acquainted with my father, the commanding officer was well aware that we hated the Russians as much as he did. The officer knew that our family would probably be driven out of Latvia by the Soviets, so he offered to let our family stay on his farm near Eckernförde if we needed a temporary refuge. The Germans eventually drove the Russians out of Latvia; so one occupation was followed by another. Now it was Germany's turn to act as oppressors until 1944.

THE RETURN OF THE COMMUNISTS TO LATVIA

In 1944, heavy fighting took place in Latvia between German and Soviet troops. Two hundred thousand German and Latvian troops were trapped in Courland between the Baltic Sea and the Soviet lines. Hitler refused their commanding officer's request to be evacuated. The Army Group Courland held out until May 1945, but many of the troops were captured by the Soviets and sent to prison camps. By May 1945, Riga was recaptured, and Latvia was again under Soviet control.

With the German retreat and return of the Communists, we knew that we could not live under Soviet rule, and we decided to flee Latvia. It was a painful decision because some of our neighbors thought we should stay and help fight the Russians. Others knew there was little chance of holding off such a large force, and they understood the decision my parents made.

Even though it meant losing our farm and everything we had worked for, leaving Latvia would at least give us a chance to live in freedom. Nothing matched my parents' dread and hatred of the

Soviets. We had witnessed the mass deportation and murder of fellow Latvians during the first occupation. After the defeat of the Germans, the Soviets renewed their persecution of any Latvian who they felt might resist their rule. They imprisoned and deported over sixty-five thousand Latvians—landowners, government officials, and other "intelligentsia." The Soviet plan called for total takeover of all land and property. Our property would become part of a large "collective farm" run by the Communists. Farmers would not be allowed to keep their profits, or make any decisions about their land. Another order called for forced intermarriages between Latvian women and Russian soldiers. Since the Germans conscripted thousands of Latvian men, many of whom lost their lives while fighting losing battles in Russia, many unmarried or widowed Latvian women remained. The Russians ordered many of these women to marry their soldiers. Later in my life on my athletic trips to Europe as a Nike representative for nearly twenty years, I met many athletes from Latvia who had Latvian first names, but Russian last names. A typical Latvian today might have a first name Janis (John) with a last name Korchenkow.

Russian became the official language. Latvian customs and festivals were curtailed or eliminated. Despite years of occupation, the Soviets only partially succeeded in eliminating Latvian culture. They failed to destroy our spirit, our institutions, our work ethic, our pride in accomplishment, or our religious institutions. Since independence in 1918, Latvian literacy stood at 98 percent, one of the highest in Europe. At one time it was the second largest (per capita) European publisher of books. Only during Latvia's independence, between the two World Wars, have the Latvian people had an opportunity to speak for themselves. Today Latvia has regained its independence and is slowly rebuilding its economy. Just this year (2015) Latvia was able to join the European Common Market and was granted membership in NATO. All of the national leaders once again are Latvians. The spark for independence, starting with the overthrow of Soviet rule by the Estonians, became known as the "Singing Revolution." In a similar way, Latvia followed with its own massive uprising and became free of brutal Soviet rule. Sixty years later, the sons and daughters who were not born in Latvia, and who are now scattered around the world, are left in a quandary about their new identity. Numerous people have returned home to be re-united with lost relatives, while others are discovering a new Latvian spirit in exile. One such Latvian, *Janis Jaunsudrabins,* said it best:

"As much as we identify with our Latvian roots—feeling at home in Latvia with our relatives, seeing the sights we learned about as children, "growing up Latvian" in a country strange to our parents, the joy of being able to visit the land of our heritage can't erase the bittersweet knowledge that we should have been born and raised in a free Latvia. For our parents passed their pain of separation on to us—an unfathomable loss, real and palpable. But more important and valuable, they passed on the love of their country and heritage."

ABANDONING OUR FARM (1944)

On a cold day in 1944, we made a decision to leave the beautiful farm that we had loved so much. The Soviets were advancing, getting closer with each hour. The sounds of the rumbling tanks created widespread terror. The ground trembled, and birds flew in all directions. The boom of German guns, however, was becoming fainter each day, and we knew that the Germans were retreating. With gunfire coming from two directions, we doubted if we would survive. It was becoming more urgent to make a move or perish in the crossfire. We were hoping that my uncle would join us, so we could escape together. He never showed up at our prearranged meeting place, and we later learned that he was intercepted by the Russians and forcibly returned to his farm. His family was lined up behind the barn and shot.

We had only a few hours to gather our belongings before fleeing our farm. My parents didn't own expensive jewelry, but they did have some amber, which could be made into rings and bracelets. Above all, the material could be exchanged for other items we knew we would eventually need.

We quickly gathered up anything of immediate value that would keep during our journey, such as smoked hams and salami and dried fruit. Of course, we also tried to salvage any family pictures that we could. We packed everything we could carry onto a horse-drawn carriage. We didn't know how long our journey would take or which route would be safest. For me, the worst part of our decision to abandon the farm was leaving Rex behind. Rex sensed that we would be disappearing, and it took the life out of both of us. My saddest memory is that of Rex following behind our carriage until he realized that he could not join us. The last time I saw my dog, he had stopped walking and was lying on the road with his head tucked between his legs.

Our goal was to reach the seaport of Liepaja, where we hoped to board a boat that would take us to a safe country. We knew that the Russians were advancing in our direction, so we spent the first night in the woods. The next morning we were awakened by cannon fire of the retreating Germans and advancing Russians. It became our most reliable indicator of how close the troops were.

After a few days, other Latvian families joined us, creating a caravan on the roads heading south. We had become easy targets for the Russian planes that appeared suddenly from behind the clouds to strafe the roads. When we spotted the Russian fighters, we dove for cover in ditches and behind trees. The sight of the fighters swooping down on us was chilling and something that I will never forget. When they turned out of their sleek dives and headed straight at us, our hearts stopped. Movies depicting World War II fighters exchanging gunfire while screaming through the air still give me chills. We were unwilling witnesses to all-out air battles, with numerous planes trailing smoke and twisting as they plunged to earth. Roads became clogged with dead horses, broken-down carriages, and overturned wagons. People were carrying whatever personal belongings they still had, knowing how important they would become for their survival. We were lucky to survive close calls on the road, but many other families suffered tragic losses. We rested most nights in the woods, giving our horses a place to feed and recover. We were thankful for the friendly farmers who provided us with food and shelter. We admired their courage and determination to remain in their mother country, knowing that they might eventually lose everything to the Russians.

Children cried hysterically while clinging to their parents. The lines extended to the horizon: an endless procession of sad faces and spent bodies. We were sometimes so exhausted that we were ready to give up hope. After nearly two weeks of evading the Russians, we arrived at the seaport town of Liepaja on the Baltic Sea. My father spent two days in a futile search for a ship that would take our family to a safe port. He begged several captains to let our family board their ships, but they all refused. The captains informed my father that it was still not safe to leave Liepaja, because Russian submarines were sinking ships as they sailed from the harbor.

My father heard of one ship captain who visited Latvian ports and respected Latvian people. This captain provided our last chance for escape. My father anticipated that he might need some bargaining leverage, so he brought some bottles of vodka to entice the captain to reconsider. Wartime shortages had made alcohol a valuable commodity, and my father offered it to convince the captain of a cargo ship heading to the German port of Danzig to let our family board. The vodka turned out to be our lifesaver, since this was the last ship to leave Latvia that day.

As we were leaving, Russian planes attacked the harbor and left the city in flames. The captain was able to evade a Russian submarine that was chasing exiting ships, and we arrived in Danzig the next morning. We had escaped Latvia.

During this period, it is estimated that over two hundred thousand Latvians successfully escaped, mostly to central Europe. However, many who escaped to Sweden were forcibly returned to Latvia, since Sweden had a treaty with Russia calling for repatriation of former Soviet citizens.

5. Refugees boarding ship in Ventspils, Latvia, 1944.

REFUGEES (1944–49)

DANZIG, GERMANY - NOVEMBER 1944

We arrived in Danzig in the early morning darkness. We had mixed feelings: we were haunted by guilt for abandoning our homeland, and we felt relief that we were gaining our freedom. The dark and cold of Danzig did little to elevate our spirits. We were pinning our hopes for a new life on a country where we knew no one and didn't understand the language. We had given up everything we were familiar with in order to escape Latvia. We felt that we would probably never again be able to see our beloved homeland. It was difficult to overcome our feelings of helplessness: we were now refugees and at the mercy of strangers. Because of the unexpected hordes of Eastern Europeans attempting to escape the Russian forces, the Germans had set up makeshift camps wherever there was space. Our lodging was in an abandoned building. There were no rooms, only spaces within the building separated by blankets, sheets, or flimsy wood panels. Our small partitioned area had two bunk beds with three levels each, one table, 2 chairs, and a locker. The room next to ours was the biggest partition in the building, and was reserved for religious services. I enjoyed the Greek Orthodox services, which featured a choir. I remember an amazing male bass voice booming out "Gospajie pa milo" songs, (Russian religious chants). There was no central heating, which forced all of us to wear every piece of clothing we had carried with us.

Most of our fellow refugees were Eastern Europeans, including Russians. They came from all walks of life: farmers, landowners, government officials, writers, artists, and intellectuals. You could recognize former military personnel because they had cut off buttons from the epaulets of their uniforms. They thought that their status as former military personnel might work against them. We were joined by Russian Orthodox priests and their families, Polish fathers carrying children on their backs, as well as well-dressed people with expensive suitcases. The refugees were huddled together like penguins in an Arctic storm, with each group speaking a different language, most of which we were unable to understand. Everyone wore hats, coats, and shawls brought from their homeland, but everyone still shivered in the penetrating cold. Bundled up in makeshift layers of clothing, we settled down in our cramped quarters for what we hoped would be a short stay.

Life in the refugee camp was a virtual hell, but at least we were alive. We depended on the dwindling supplies of food the Germans were able to provide. We survived mainly on black bread, potato-peelings and vegetable soups, watered-down oat mush, as well as the remaining food that we had carried from home. There was no meat, milk, fruit, or eggs. The few infirmaries were filled with sick refugees. I became ill with Russian typhoid fever, which my cardiologist recently diagnosed as the origin of my current heart problems. If my father hadn't carried me on his back to a local hospital, I likely would not have made it in the camp. My survival during that period can be attributed to my father exchanging some of the amber that we had salvaged from our farm.

My parents did everything they could to keep our spirits up. My mother told stories of the wonderful moments we had all enjoyed on our farm, and she assured us that we could look forward to better days. They sacrificed everything they had worked for to escape the Russians, so we needed to stay strong and confident that we would make better lives for ourselves. By reading Latvian books that we carried with us, we were allowed to return, for brief moments, to our homeland. We joined other Latvians and kept up our morale by singing folk tunes and sharing stories about the homeland.

If we had remained in Latvia, we would have had little hope. The previous Russian occupation was marked by persecution and constant threat of exile to Siberia. At least our escape was successful. It provided us with some optimism that we could endure other hardships.

After a month in the refugee camp, we heard reports that the Russians were rapidly advancing west. If they found us, we would probably be returned as prisoners to Russia or Latvia. We gathered our meager belongings and fled. We sought out the farm of the German officer who my father had befriended back in Latvia. We took a train to Kiel to seek out the officer's farm in nearby Eckernförde. We found the estate but learned that the officer had been killed at the Russian front. However, after we discussed our relationship with the officer and our mutual hatred of the Russians, his family offered to shelter us. The officer's wife and children fixed up their guesthouse, which would be our home for the next six months. The only thing we had to show our appreciation for their kindness was one of the amber-embedded candleholders that we had carried from Latvia. Their estate was near a village, and we tried our best to become anonymous by quietly embedding ourselves in the life of the community. It was a challenging time, since most people in the village had not conceded defeat and still supported Hitler. We watched a number of night rallies and heard the Horst-Wessel-Lied, the notorious Nazi jingoistic anthem, sung exuberantly by our neighbors. We grew accustomed to seeing the outstretched hands of the Nazi salute during the rallies. It was difficult to avoid hearing Hitler's rants on the radio.

We watched the spectacle of almost daily bombing runs over Kiel, with British planes flying at night and Americans during the day. At first, the German searchlights were able to light up the night sky, illuminating targets for antiaircraft fire. But soon, the searchlight installations were destroyed, and the bombing raids proceeded with the planes no longer required to dodge German antiaircraft fire.

My brother was approaching the age when German boys were required to join Hitler Youth. Modris was pressured to participate, but my parents stalled long enough for the townspeople to realize that the war was almost lost and one more Hitler youth wasn't going to make a difference.

During our stay on the Eckernförde estate, we had maintained contact with other Latvian refugees. We knew that we had a limited time to remain in Eckernförde, so we made plans to flee to another part of Germany. Our Latvian contacts warned us that we needed to be careful about which part of Germany we traveled to. We heard rumors that in the event of Allied victory, the northern part of Germany would become under British jurisdiction. Since the British were still allied to Russia and agreed to repatriate Russian citizens, we were worried that we could be forcibly returned to Latvia. The Allied leaders at the Yalta Conference, including the United States, agreed to forcefully repatriate refugees to the Soviet Union. Since we were still considered Soviet citizens, we knew we must attempt to leave northern Germany. Eventually, the United States changed its policy and opposed forced repatriation. Our goal was to reach southern Germany, which was destined to become the American zone. Underground communication was making it clear that it was urgent to try to get to Regensburg, which would be under the control of the Americans. Western relief organizations were setting up refugee camps and attempting to find western countries that would be willing to accept Eastern European refugees.

We would need to board a train to Hamburg, one of the few rail routes still in operation. However, as soon as we arrived in Hamburg, the city became a prime target for Allied bombing. We were stuck, having no choice but to flee to bomb shelters during the raids. We dreaded hearing the sirens, for that meant that we would soon hear the terrifying whistle of bombs falling on the city. The whistles were followed by powerful explosions, which destroyed the beautiful buildings that we had recently walked past. The bombs also destroyed much of the railroad lines, so we were worried that we would be stranded in Hamburg. Crews worked feverishly, filling in bomb craters and repairing bridges, but we were unable to travel south for several days. Finally, we heard the long blasts of the locomotive whistles, and we boarded a heavily loaded train that moved slowly out of Hamburg. We were indeed fortunate to be on our way to southern Germany.

The war was almost over, and American ground forces were approaching. I'll never forget the sight of convoys of American trucks. They stopped and opened the back gates, and American soldiers jumped out. We were delighted to see the Yanks, who greeted us with so much enthusiasm. My parents cried openly, realizing that we were finally liberated. It was the first time we had come in contact with blacks of any nationality. Years later, when I taught American history, I took great pride in pointing out how President Truman ended segregation of the military.

ARRIVING IN REGENSBURG DISPLACED PERSONS CAMP (MAY 1945)

The war had taken a heavy toll on German cities with any strategic importance. American bombing raids had destroyed rail lines, power plants, and factories. Most buildings were either destroyed or had gaping holes in the walls that remained standing. It was as if some great monster had ripped them open to gaze inside. Ancient roofs and Gothic domes of churches had been turned into rubble.

Our first camp was in the Bavarian city of Regensburg, around which the Danube River curved gracefully, providing stark contrast to the bomb-ravaged buildings. Upon arrival at our new camp, we were ordered to go to former German military barracks that had been partially destroyed by Allied bombs. Despite the reminders of war that surrounded us, we were relieved to find a place where we felt safe. Our living conditions were basic, but were made easier to tolerate knowing that it was temporary.

We lived among hundreds of other Baltic (Latvian, Lithuanian, and Estonian) families in the camps. The camps were organized by American relief organizations and the United Nations Relief and Rehabilitation Administration (UNRRA). There were some camps in the British and French zones, but most were in the American zone. Refugees were housed in whatever buildings were available: army barracks, abandoned factories, or schools. Latvians were placed in five camps of varying size. Sometimes the camps were in use for a few months, while others were home to refugees for five years.

As more Eastern Europeans were repatriated, we were moved to other camps in order to consolidate the remaining refugees. We never knew how long we would stay in a camp, so we were always prepared for a hasty exit. We were aware of the fact that the DP camps were temporary, with the deadline for closing all camps set for 1949. If we could not find a sponsor in another country or find a home in Germany, we would be sent back to Latvia or Russia, which would be essentially the same thing. If we were sent back to Latvia, we could end up as common laborers on the farm we once owned. If we didn't make a move within a year, there would no longer be any DP camps left for us.

In some ways, we appreciated how simple our lives had become: we had few worries such as mortgages or car payments. Our main concern was always food; camp food was monotonously bland, and there was never enough to fill us. Our rooms provided little privacy. In many cases, hanging blankets or half walls were the only structures separating families. The UNRRA and other organizations were in charge of distributing shoes, medicine, toiletries, and clothing to refugees. The central heating systems frequently failed, which meant that staying warm during the frigid German winters would prove to be our greatest challenge.

We were assigned to camps in which most of the other occupants were Latvians, which we felt was a blessing. The camp chose its own leaders, who organized schools, church services, concerts, and folk dancing, all of which made our lives bearable. We were fortunate to be able to continue school. Former teachers volunteered to teach English, math, some sciences, music, art, and German. The American Junior Red Cross supplied our classrooms with basic materials. Each of us received a pencil and sheet of blank paper, which we were told would need to last the entire school day. We learned how to gently erase each day's written work, carefully avoiding scratching holes in the paper. Detailed report cards were issued, showing number grades (2 for poor, 3–4, and 5 being the best). In addition to the core subjects, we also received grades for singing, drawing, neatness (orderliness), speech, and overall behavior (deportment). My parents saved my report card and carried it with us to America.

6. Displaced persons camp – Regensburg, Germany, 1945.

Latvians love singing traditional tunes, so many joined a choir. A rudimentary library, stocked with books that the refugees carried from home, was set up near the school. Boy Scout and stamp clubs were also popular. We published newsletters and constructed photo displays that became a testament to our survival. We also enjoyed sports, so volleyball and soccer games attracted many participants. I was happy that cross-country races were held for young runners.

Following our one-year stay in Regensburg, we were moved to Ingolstadt, also on the Danube River. We were eventually transferred to Esslingen, and finally to Neustadt, near Frankfurt. Latvians had always taken great pride in leaving premises as clean as they found them. In all the camps where we stayed, our barracks were left as clean and neat as humanly possible. Floors and windows were scrubbed clean, no trash was left behind, eating utensils and pots and pans were polished, and blankets and sheets were washed, cleaned, and folded. American officials were amazed that we Latvians would work so diligently and with such a spirited attitude to leave temporary barracks in such great shape. We were told that we were the only nationality that took such pride.

The Latvian people held on to a faint hope of returning to Latvia, but were forced to face the reality that Russia had taken over Eastern Europe, which all but eliminated that chance. We all had to overcome many barriers in our attempts to find countries that would accept refugees. Britain, for example, accepted only single men who would agree to work in coal mines. Canada accepted young and middle-aged women who would work in households, whereas Australia wanted entire families, including children. The United States required a sponsor who would agree to take whole families and who would be willing to look after them until they could survive on their own. We hoped to go to the United States. However, we didn't expect to spend five years moving between various camps before a sponsor could be found.

In 1949, we received notice that a farmer from the state of Washington, Mr. Brodahl, with the help of the Lutheran Church, had agreed to sponsor our family. During this time, an additional twenty to forty thousand fortunate Latvians were also selected to immigrate to the United States. The selection process was riddled with delays due to the need for careful screening of all refugees. We were required to submit detailed records of our background, past political status, and health history. Over one hundred thousand refugees from other Eastern European nations were rejected because of suspicious political associations or a history of contagious diseases, especially tuberculosis. Their only choice was to locate a home in Germany or return to their native lands.

While in Regensburg, we were allowed to leave our camp and go into the city, which had suffered extensive damage from bombing raids. Parts of the city, however, began showing signs of recovery. Small stores finally had food to sell, and after the rubble was cleared, some streets came to life with the reopening of cafes.

After the war had ended, the Allies—Americans, French, and British—were faced with the ominous task of reconstructing Germany. This humanitarian effort was meant to show local populations that America cared about their future. American troops occupied southern Germany and helped with recovery by providing food stamps and maintaining overall law and order. Local German police were given the responsibility of handling local problems.

We received some spending money, which we used for buying inexpensive toys, postcards, ice cream and sodas, or for taking short trips outside of the camp. Our favorite excursion was a boat ride down the Danube River. I had been fascinated with rivers ever since my boyhood on the farm, but I had never experienced a carefree ride on a leisure boat. One visitor observed that, "It felt as carefree as a leaf floating on water." The river, nearly fifty yards wide at places, snaked through the city on its way to northern Germany. We saw abandoned castles peering from steep cliffs high above the river. We ventured east as far as the medieval city of Passau, which had been spared from Allied bombing. It was the last stop before entering Austria.

Thinking about it today, the Danube was the only neutral body traversing through so many war-torn countries, so it was spared from much of the bombing. The river was always full of long lines of boats and huge barges carrying coal and foodstuffs, each sliding past the other in slow motion, like sleepy alligators. We studied each barge's name and flags, and made a game out of guessing where it was headed or where it had begun its journey.

Our opportunities to participate in sports and cultural events expanded during this period, giving us a welcome diversion from the monotony of camp life. Modris and Jausma joined me on the track and field team. Modris excelled at sprints, and Jausma usually won the throwing events. I was excited about cross-country races. I felt confident that I could do well, since running had come so easily for me on the farm. The community organizers had fun designing challenging race courses. They made all runners jump logs and negotiate hills and mud before reaching the finish line. I started slowly, not sure how to pace myself. I had not run since leaving Latvia, so I was content following the main group. Half way through the race I started to pass those who started too fast. Still feeling relaxed, my confidence grew with each step and I kept passing one runner after another. We had already run through the muddy part, which left our shoes dirty with only the menacing and slippery log remaining. The finish line was only a short distance away, I jumped the log high enough, clearing it with ease. I turned around to see the others still clearing the log. With nobody else in front of me I knew I had won my first competitive race. From then on I knew that running was in my blood.

My father applied for a job working with the US Labor Service at a nearby military supply depot. Having military experience in Latvia helped him to establish good rapport with the officers. Eventually he met General Lucius Clay, the Allied Commander for Europe, who was impressed with my father's background. Years later, when my father worked for the Continental Can Company in Seattle, he met the general again. The general had become the CEO of another company and was touring the Seattle plant. He recognized my father immediately from the displaced persons camps, calling him "Walt" (short for Voldemars), and the two enjoyed a warm reunion. From that day forward, my father's fellow workers at Continental treated him with increased respect, even if he was only a "maintenance engineer" (a janitor).

7. Danube River outing. From left; Modris, Atis, Jausma and Vera, 1947.

SAILING TO AMERICA (MAY 1949)

Certain events stand out in one's life. The sight of Rex sadly following our carriage as we left our farm, the shared terror of bombing raids, and the whine of Russian planes diving toward us as we fled to the west all remain vivid images in my mind. Less traumatic but nonetheless memorable was listening to Germans singing the stirring Horst-Wessel-Lied, winning my first cross-country race, and boat excursions along the Danube with my family. None of these, however, compared to the sheer joy my family and I felt when we saw the Statue of Liberty for the first time.

Living in limbo for five years took a toll on all of us, but we remained optimistic that one day we would set foot on American soil. It was truly a glorious moment when we received documents for departure to the United States. We traveled first to the seaport city of Bremerhaven, where we would be processed for passage on a refugee ship sailing for New York. On the train ride north, we observed the near-total destruction of German cities (Nuremberg, Cologne, Düsseldorf). We especially remember that the only structure still standing in Cologne was the huge medieval cathedral.

Upon arrival in Bremerhaven, we were given another health examination along with numerous shots. Both of my arms were sore for days. As we waited to board our ship, we joined a long line of refugees from Eastern Europe, most of which were desperately clutching their possessions as they pushed each other and shouted in strange languages. The decks were crowded with people of every age, class, and nationality. A majority had simply put whatever belongings they had in tattered suitcases or cloth bags. Many were Jews from Russia, whose long beards and black hats made them stand out from the Lithuanians, Poles, and Hungarians. Although we didn't see them until it was time to disembark, we recognized well-to-do families by their fine clothes and expensive leather suitcases. They had purchased the best lodging on the top decks, out of sight from the rest of us. Since the captain's payment was determined by how many bodies could be crowded together, every space on the ship was occupied with refugees.

The eleven-day voyage across the Atlantic was difficult from the beginning. We were packed like sardines into small stalls. We all had to tolerate other nationalities' food smells and body odors. Since most of the passengers were unaccustomed to the rough seas of the North Atlantic, many became seasick. The smell of vomit, urine and feces permeated our living quarters. The small cots, along with the frequent fire and emergency drills, made it difficult to sleep. We were sometimes forced to go out on the decks during the coldest of gales. Many of us felt the after-effects of multiple shots that we received before leaving Germany. Both of my arms were swollen, making it difficult to sleep. Just when we thought the voyage would never end, we received news that we were approaching New York. We knew it would be a matter of hours before we would catch our first glimpse of the Statue of Liberty. Our fellow passengers suddenly seemed much friendlier. Conversations about illness and misery were replaced by predictions of health and prosperity in our new land. As we sailed into the harbor, people in the front of the ship became excited, raising their hands and pointing to something that was appearing through the fog. When fog cleared, strangers were seen embracing, shaking hands, and striking up songs as we glided past the Statute of Liberty. Some just shouted a simple word, "Amerika!" The skyline of New York City was awe-inspiring. The multicolored buildings staring down at us were the tallest that we had ever seen. It was as if the dark, depressing black-and-white images of war-ravaged Europe had suddenly been replaced by a brilliantly alive Technicolor landscape.

AMERICA, AT LAST!

Unlike previous refugees, who first came into contact with America through Ellis Island and who had to endure an arduous and lengthy processing ritual, ours was a simple, one-day process. We were given the same shots that we had already received in Bremerhaven (no arguments: double "Ouch!"), along with proper documents and enough money for our rail transport to our new home in Washington. Our train was scheduled to leave in a few hours, so we decided to use the time for our first walk through American streets. New York was a huge and exciting place. We had left behind bombed-out cities, inhabited by distraught people, walking aimlessly and dressed in rags. We had memories of people carrying all their worldly belongings in a sack, having lost their homes, relatives, and way of life. Those images could not be easily erased as we took our first walk through the streets of New York.

We gazed in shock as we raised our heads and strained to see the tops of the buildings, which seemed to disappear into the sky. The sound of the multitudes of cars and buses was completely new and captivated our imagination. Where were they all going in such a hurry? We saw small shops everywhere, along with food wagons parked along the side of the street. It had been years since we had seen so much fresh food. Although we didn't understand what the vendors were saying, we knew they were trying to entice pass-ersby to stop and purchase their wares. Restaurants were crowded with people, many of whom spoke languages other than English. It was our first exposure to the American melting pot. The smells and sights of the food from street vendors woke our dormant taste buds. We were aching to try some of the delicious-looking food. Since we had been given some pocket money, we decided that a first taste of American food would be an appropriate way to celebrate our arriv-al. We noticed a young couple with two children happily eating ice cream from paper containers. We hadn't eaten sweets in years and couldn't resist joining them. There was no shortage of vendors sell-ing every imaginable dessert, but we had to make a quick choice, since our time was limited. I gazed at the variety of containers in the display cabinet and tried to decipher the labels. Not knowing which to pick, I pointed randomly at one of the cups. The young saleslady gave me a strange look, as if questioning my choice. I got strange stares from the nearby children as the saleslady proceeded to pick the coins from my outstretched hand. I removed the cover from the container and started eating. After a small taste, I knew my first bite of American food wasn't ice cream, but cottage cheese. I ate the entire cup with a smile on my face, hoping everyone around me would think that cottage cheese was, indeed, my choice all along. That was the first of many goofy mistakes I would make as I learned the strange language and new ways of America.

JOURNEY TO WASHINGTON

Although we couldn't read our tickets, we were told that we would be traveling by train to Washington. We had no idea that there was a difference between Washington, DC, and the state of Washington. We assumed that we would be enjoying a short (according to the map we had received) train ride to Washington, DC. We passed small towns and stretches of woods that reminded us of Europe. We also got our first looks at huge horse-breeding estates surrounded by immaculate white fences. The views of serene countryside were usually followed by scenes of dark soot emanating from smoke-stacks of large factories on the outskirts of cities. We were encour-aged to see so many well-built roads and the impressive variety of cars they carried. We wondered what kind of automobile we would end up buying.

Night settled in, and we wondered why we had not yet arrived in our nation's capital. We purchased some sandwiches for dinner and stretched out on the wooden seats to try to sleep. The next morning, we showed the conductor our tickets. He calmly informed us that our final destination was a West Coast city named Seattle, in the state of Washington. We learned that we would not be travel-ing to Washington, DC. We took another look at our map and saw Washington State on the other side of the country. We then realized that we had a three-day journey ahead of us.

Our journey across America would traverse three different time zones and numerous states, all of which were just strange names on a map. We crossed countless bridges, followed beautiful winding rivers, and made stops in the larger cities. We were befriended by our conductor, an immigrant from Ireland, which helped to reduce the stress of a long journey in a strange land. He made sure we un-derstood how long we would have for each stop, so we would have a chance to get off of the train and stretch our legs. Unfortunately, his job ended in Chicago, which he explained had many industries and was inhabited by immigrants like us. We were sad to see him get off our train, but the help he had provided made the rest of the journey easier. We had a long layover in Chicago, so we had a chance to see some sights and enjoy fresh food before continuing our journey. My father picked up discarded newspapers, hoping to gain some insight as to what was happening in the rest of the world. He gleaned enough from the headlines and pictures to get a basic understanding of world events. He loved learning and urged us to try to master our new language as quickly as possible. Wading through newspapers and watching news reports on television helped in this effort. My father eventually became an avid reader of *The Seattle Times* and *Time* magazine.

After leaving Chicago, we traversed miles and miles of flat farmland. Corn and wheat fields, seldom interrupted by the woods that were so familiar to us in the farmlands of Latvia, extended to the horizon. My father couldn't believe that such massive tracts of land were devoted to growing one crop. The farms were often bisected by paved, ramrod-straight roads. We were almost hypnotized by the long hours of staring at the monotonous landscape. Since the flat prairie was seemingly unending, we wondered if this was the same countryside that we would encounter in Seattle.

On the morning of our third day of travel, we looked out the window and saw trees and rolling hills. We were elated to leave the unbroken horizon of the plains behind. The rolling hills gradually became mountains, and we saw cowboys riding herd as cattle roamed over large tracts of grazing land. Our train struggled up switch-backed slopes before traversing seven-thousand-foot passes in the Rocky Mountains. The tracks cut through granite outcroppings with interspersed patches of grass and groves of stunted pines. Hawks could be seen floating in the mountain thermals as our train crawled along a trestle that traversed a deep gorge. The views were spectacular, as if each mile we traveled was like turning a page in a picture book. After clearing the top of a ridge, the tracks meandered alongside rivers with clear blue water rushing over falls. We saw fisherman wading in streams and gracefully casting their lines into swirling pools. Modris, Jausma, and I made a game of counting the number of tunnels the train had to go through and guessing the time it would take to clear each one. We saw the snow of cone-shaped peaks in the distance. We were approaching the Cascade Range, and by this time, we knew that Seattle was somewhere on the other side. We were reaching the end of our journey. Even though we were exhausted from the long ride, we were elated to finally arrive in Seattle.

WASHINGTON (1949-53)

ARRIVAL IN FERDALE—1949

The minute we stepped off the train we spotted our sponsor, Mr. Fred Brodahl, who welcomed us with a smile and a warm embrace. No words were spoken, the joy of arrival was written on all of our faces. We gathered our belongings and boarded a mini-bus that he had borrowed from a neighbor. We drove north to Ferndale, a small town close to the Canadian border which painted a picture of beautiful countryside with the picturesque Puget Sound on one side and the snow-covered Mt Baker and the Cascade on the other side. As we got closer, I noticed a water tower with the letters FERNDALE clearly visible from the road. We knew we had finally arrived at our new home. It was a small town, located only six miles from the Canadian border. Its main street had some restaurants, a hardware store that was next to a JCPenney store. On the other side of the street, the Bank of America stood out by itself, flanked by antiques stores. A friendly atmosphere could be felt by strolling the main street, with people openly greeting each other, as if they had known each other for a long time. In 1949, it was the major road between Seattle and Vancouver BC. Today, Interstate 5 runs along the town, with most drivers hardly paying attention to it. The country roads throughout the county were still unpaved, producing a lot of dust and tire wear. Most of the people in Ferndale had medium-sized farms, similar to ours in Latvia. They were mainly involved with dairy and truck farming, alfalfa production for cattle and horses.

Mr. Brodahl, who was a well-built man with an infectious smile made us welcomed to his home. Like my father, he was a hard-working Lutheran with ties going back to Norway. His wife had passed away and his son was in Europe with U.S. Air Force, who flew bombing missions over Hamburg, at the same time we were stuck in underground shelters. This was certainly some kind of an unusual coincidence. Mr. Brodahl owned a dairy farm which was a little smaller than our home in Latvia. Like our farm, it consisted of pastureland for dairy cows, but also had small areas of forest and a vegetable garden. He was more than happy to have my father help out with farm jobs, especially dairying. Ferndale would become our home for the next two years. No more refugee camps and no more worries about bombs dropping on us, only contented peace. It was a friendly neighborhood from the way neighbors exchanged greetings and honked their horns every time they passed our house. It seemed that everyone knew their neighbors and were keenly interested in meeting the newcomers. They took us to picnics and short trips to see the area.

We looked forward to attending Lutheran church services on Sundays and it didn't matter that we understood little of minister's sermon. But we could sing along with the hymns. After church services, many people stopped by to inquire more about the newly-arrived refugees.

With countless rivers and hiking trails nearby and the rainy atmosphere, no wonder it attracted people from Norway. We were comforted by the fact that our first home in America would be similar to the one we left in Latvia. Arriving at his home was such a welcome relief, no more travel, no worries about bombs falling or sparce, temporary living arrangements. Only contented peace to be in a home again, we each had our own bed to sleep in and delicious food. I quickly made friends with Mr. Brodahl's dog, who reminded me of Rex. My mother helped with the cooking and Mr. Brodahl was happy to have my father helping with farm chores, especially the daily ritual of transporting milk cans to the road for morning pick up. In order to do the job, my father had to learn to drive a jeep. Once he ended up in the ditch. Another time, while backing up the jeep to the milk stand, he mistakenly pushed the gas pedal, instead of the brake, smashing the milk can full force, milk gushing up in the air. On another day, he was apparently driving too comfortable because a police officer cited him for driving too slow. My mother preferred to sit in the back of the car, making my dad nervous with her constant unsolicited advice. On one drive to a picnic, my father had heard enough commentary from the back seat and slammed on the brakes. The cake resting on my mother's lap flew forward and decorated the front seat and my dad's own lap.

8. The Petersons family on the Brodahl farm in Washington.
From left; Jausma, Modris, Mr. Brodahl, Atis, Voldemars and Vera, 1959.

Try as we did, learning English was slow and difficult. When Mr. Brodahl asked me to go to the barn and fetch a wrench, I brought him a hammer. I replied "yes" to questions that should have been answered a "no". I thought yes sounded more polite than no. Although we didn't understand everything that was said, we loved listening to Mr. Brodahl's brother tell stories about his fishing trips to Alaska. He described what it was like to haul a forty-pound salmon out of the freezing water of the Arctic sea. Whenever he returned to Ferndale, he brought salmon with him. It was the first time we had tasted fresh salmon and I considered it a treat. Salmon remains one of my favorite meals today.

We were fortunate that our first home was the Brodahl's farm. It provided a secure and wholesome introduction to American culture. At the end of our stay in Ferndale, we felt less "foreign". My father helped with the church bookkeeping duties, something he did in Latvia as well. Neighbors often stopped by, bringing pies and sharing with us pictures of parents and relatives who had emigrated from Scandinavia. They took us on picnics and short sightseeing trips around Ferndale. We visited Birch Bay, on beautiful Puget Sound. During low tides, we could walk out one hundred yards on its long beach before getting our feet wet. We gazed at the spectacular snow-packed Mount Baker, at ten thousand foot in the Cascade, which became a familiar sight, especially during the winter months. It was a hikers and fishermen paradise with so many trails and running streams full of trout.

Remembering our stay with Mr. Brodahl and meeting such friendly people gave us such a wonderful insight as to what America was all about. We found Americans to be the hardest working and unusually hospitable people. No wonder so many foreigners wished to come to America. These were the cream of the crop from so many lands, losing everything they had, but willing to start a new life. Their courage has certainly made a huge contribution.

RELOCATING TO EASTERN WASHINGTON (AUGUST 1950)

Our two-year stay on the Brodahl farm was designed to provide us with the confidence and skills to become a self-sufficient family unit once again. Mr. Brodahl gave my father an excellent recommendation, and he was hired to supervise agricultural irrigation in the eastern Washington town of Prosser. His employer arranged for us to rent a house just outside of town at a reasonable price. Prosser, located in the Tri-cities area near Pasco and Kennewick, was about the same size as Ferndale.

The climate in eastern Washington was more extreme than what we were accustomed to in Ferndale. It was hotter and dryer during the summer and colder in the winter. We missed the lush, green forests and proximity to the ocean that we enjoyed in western Washington. Just when I was getting used to my Ferndale school and enjoying my newly acquired friendships, we had to go through another period of acclimation in Prosser.

As soon as we arrived, we could see that the Prosser community was centered on agriculture. We noticed farmers in overalls driving small pickups. They came into town, picked up supplies at the local hardware or farm outlet stores, and grabbed a quick meal at Denny's. My dad's job in the agricultural fields was demanding, requiring long hours of intensive labor. Each day, from dawn to dusk, he dismantled long aluminum pipes at one location and assembled them in another. It was grueling labor, especially in the hundred-degree summer heat. The ten-hour days, six days a week took a heavy toll on his mind and body. He was accustomed to doing similar work in Latvia, but his labors were for the benefit of our own farm. As an immigrant who spoke little English, he would have to get used to minimum-wage jobs. For a man with extensive skills and experience, it was a blow to his pride.

We got summer jobs to supplement my father's income. I picked strawberries, Modris worked the hay fields, and Jausma picked fruit.

My mother found part-time jobs in our neighborhood. I was able to experience my first bike ride during that summer. After watching a neighbor's son, Gary, ride his bike back and forth on our street, I knew I had to own one. Gary insisted that I learn how to take the bike apart and put it back together again. He taught me how to use the brakes and execute safe turns, hopefully without falling. Despite his tutelage, I still fell and had plenty of bruises to show for my efforts. When I wasn't riding a bike, our family took walks into the city, and my parents treated us to ice cream.

Prosser was located near the Hanford Nuclear Plant, which was a major production site of the uranium isotopes that fueled the US nuclear energy program. Unfortunately, Hanford was also the site of accidents that released radioactive particles into the atmosphere. During the 1950s, the scientific community was just beginning to gather information about the long-term health effects of such releases. The eventual disclosure of secret documents created new controversy about how much the government knew about those releases. Some say it was done intentionally in order to measure the effect of radiation on human populations.

Modris and Jausma worked in the fields during that time, and it is difficult to determine with certainty how much the exposure affected their health. Sadly, Modris died of cancer in 1985, and Jausma was diagnosed with thyroid cancer in 2012. Today, I am required to take daily thyroid medication. We all played and worked in an area that later was designated as restricted, but it is nevertheless difficult to prove that Hanford emissions caused our health problems.

RETURN TO SEATTLE (JUNE 1951)

Our stay in Prosser proved to be short-lived. With the help of our friends in the Lutheran church in Seattle, my father received an offer to work for Continental Can Company. The job would provide better pay and shorter hours, all with considerably less strain on my father's body. We were excited by the prospect of returning to more familiar surroundings. We had saved enough money for a down payment on a home overlooking Union Bay. Besides being close to our new schools, it had a nice garden and several fruit trees. I entered Lincoln High School as a sophomore. Lincoln enrolled about one thousand students and was located near picturesque Green Lake, a fifteen-minute ride from our home. Lincoln was larger than any school in Prosser. Although my English had improved, I still experienced the anxiety of entering a new school. As in Prosser, my teachers were tolerant and patient, and I soon felt confident about making friends and succeeding in class. It was difficult for people to get used to calling me "Atis" so I took on the American name "Pete". I also learned that part of the ritual of making friends and fitting in was easier if you had access to or owned a car. I was determined to have a car of my own. Although financial constraints limited my choices, I settled on a dark blue 1949 Ford. I think I spent more time cleaning fouled spark plugs than actually driving. Every garage attendant around Lincoln High School knew what to expect when my sputtering Ford pulled into the parking lot: pull the plugs and clean them. At first the mechanic helped me, but soon I was left to do the dirty job on my own. I could see that the old Ford would be perpetual headache, so I traded it for a '48 Chevy, a year older than the Ford but in better condition.

Despite my language problems, I adjusted to Lincoln High and soon looked forward to going to school. It helped that girls were friendly and actually noticed me. My chemistry lab partner was a beautiful girl named Dottie Provine, who later became a movie actress. German was easy for me because of my experience in the DP camps. Spelling, because it involved rote learning, was also easy, but reading was always difficult. I struggled with American literature and mathematics. Math involved learning a progression of skills, and my war-interrupted childhood put me far behind my peers. The pace of the class was too fast; by the time I learned how to master one concept, we moved to another. Our woodshop teacher kindly took me under his wing and spent extra time showing me the proper use of tools that I had never been exposed to. I enjoyed the opportunity to work with my hands and to learn a skill that I still enjoy today.

Lincoln High School had a popular and well-organized athletic program, and I was eager to participate. Football, of course, was the most popular sport, so I decided to join the team, even though I had no experience. Our football team was one of the best in Seattle, so our coach, Mr. Nolan, was surprised when I turned out in the fall of 1951. I was small and mostly ignorant of what was needed to be a good player, but Mr. Nolan, for some reason, knew I was an immigrant and admired my eagerness to be a part of the team. Because of my soccer experience, he decided to try me as a kicker. I was given jersey number "00," but my uniform did not come with shoulder pads. As a kicker who would probably never get into a game, the coaches felt that I wouldn't need them. I was at least twenty pounds lighter than most of my teammates, but they, at least, wore shoulder pads. Compared to the rest of the team, the player in jersey 00 looked like a midget. I never kicked an extra point or field goal in a game, but I accomplished one goal that my friends told me was an important part of being on the football team: the girls noticed number 00 sitting on the bench. I think they felt sorry for me, knowing that I was an immigrant.

I knew that running would be my best sport, so I looked forward to the spring term, when I could go out for the track team. I noticed a track-record board posted near our small indoor track in the basketball gymnasium.

As soon as I saw that the school record for the mile run was 4:56, I became obsessed with breaking it. I told my friends that I was going to run the next day during lunch hour, with hopes of setting a new mark. The track coach, along with many of my friends, showed up the next day to cheer me on. In my excitement, I started too fast and began to tire by the halfway point. Not wanting to disappoint those who supported me, I dug in and did my best to finish strongly. I saw the coach smiling as he stared at his watch. I had run 4:51, breaking the record by five seconds. That spring, I ran the mile and the 880-yard run, winning the Seattle City Championship in the 880.

Modris and Jausma progressed quickly with their schoolwork. Modris was a good math student, and he planned to study accounting in college. He was also an excellent sprinter in track, which earned him an athletic scholarship to Western Washington University in Bellingham. Jausma attended the University of Washington as a home economics and business major. She enjoyed studying food preparation and nutrition, and was later hired by the Seattle City Light Department. As for my future, I had to make a choice between staying in Seattle and attending the University of Washington, or heading south to California.

Seattle had an active Latvian community, with many of its members immigrating at the same time as my family. The elders of the community, including my father, built a church and social center. We took many trips to Mount Rainier, went on fishing trips in Puget Sound, attended summer camps, and participated in dance and music groups. As he did in Ferndale, my father helped with church bookkeeping and organizing volunteers. It was gratifying to belong to such a supportive and active community.

Many of the members of the Latvian community in Seattle were avid sport fishermen. Modris loved salmon fishing, so he took advantage of every opportunity to take our rowboat down to Puget Sound. I had never been fishing, and he was kind enough to let me join him for an early morning boat ride. I soon learned that fishing takes a special type of patience, a trait that I wasn't sure I possessed. I sat for hours, waiting for the telltale wiggle of the tip of my pole, a sign that a fish had taken the worm that I had so carefully threaded onto the hook. On another trip, I was jolted from my stupor when a salmon finally mouthed an anchovy. My adrenaline kicked in, and I yanked the pole toward the sky, unaware that I had also yanked the hook from the fish's mouth. By the end of our morning of fishing, Modris had landed a salmon, and I came away with a nice tan.

Modris and I were invited to become part of Seattle Track Club, which organized meets in western Washington and Canada. A number of top athletes from the University of Southern California and Whittier College spent part of their summer in Seattle. Des Koch, Russ Bonham, Rod Wilger, and Bob Lawson competed in a series of meets in the Northwest as they traveled to Victoria, BC. Many of the meets were held in conjunction with The Scottish Highland Games, which were an all-day festival. Besides track events, there were bagpipe bands playing non-stop throughout the day, along with dance competitions involving dancers dressed in kilts and native costumes. There was also caber throwing (a tall, heavy pole that had to be heaved so that it would land on the opposite end). Des Koch, the all-around USC weight man quickly mastered it and beat all the other Scottish throwers. He also entered the hurdle event whenever he noticed the hurdles were made of thin wood. Instead of hurdling over them he just crushed through them. We always checked the prizes beforehand. Often the prize for second place was more attractive than the winner's. Everyone came away with smiles on their faces having participated in such an unusual atmosphere. It was a new experience for the athletes to spend part of the summer in the cool Northwest. The Highland Games attracted athletes from all over the world, and they provided Modris and me with our first opportunity to compete in the same track meets as several well-known All-Americans, including Bob Lawson, a standout decathlete from University of Southern California. Russ Bonham's father was the coach at Whittier College, he arranged for me to get a scholarship, but The University of Washington had also offered me a scholarship, so I had a difficult decision to make. My parents urged me to stay in Seattle, where I could continue enjoying the comforts of home, be with my friends, and remain in familiar surroundings. Although I had never been to California, I had heard plenty about its sunny and mild weather. I had become tired of the constant cold and rain of Seattle, so California was alluring to me. My parents eventually supported my move, and they were happy that I would receive financial help while attending college.

CALIFORNIA (1953)

After graduating from high school and enjoying an eventful summer of track meets in Canada, weekend boat trips to Puget Sound with Bob Lawson, and fishing excursions with Modris, it was time to pack my bags. My part-time work at Continental Can Company would have to wait until next summer. It was difficult to say good-bye to my family and friends, but I planned to return home for Christmas. I threw my belongings into my Volkswagen bug and chugged off to California.

The scenic countryside of Oregon and Northern California seemed to pass quickly. Once I arrived in the Central Valley of California, I had my first looks at the vast stretches of agricultural flatlands that dominated the landscape during my second day of driving. When I finally reached Los Angeles County, I was intimidated by its size and sprawl. Seattle is a large city, but it is more compact than Los Angeles. The LA freeways were a confusing maze, and it seemed to take forever to find Whittier, a small suburb that blended in with similar communities in the southern part of Los Angeles County. Russ Bonham, who played a big part in my coming to Whittier, gave me good directions to the campus. Russ took me to the Nolan house, which would be my home during the school year. Mr. Nolan was a successful businessman and a former distance runner at Whittier, so we had a lot in common. His house was close to school, and he made sure that I was well fed. He insisted that I eat a banana every morning. I enjoyed my stay with the Nolans, and I knew that I was lucky to have his support during my freshman year.

I had no idea what classes I would take or what area I would choose for a major. I liked music, so my counselor arranged for me to take music history, solfège (reading notes), choir, English, physical fitness, and nutrition. Because I was still trying to improve my English skills, the class schedule was daunting. I was far away from home in a strange and intimidating city, so it was sometimes difficult to maintain an optimistic outlook. There were plenty of periods of frustration, but my professors and classmates were supportive. They took me to movies and the Santa Monica pier, and they treated me to hamburgers and shakes, all of which made my adjustment to college easier. Since Whittier College was founded by Quakers, we attended weekly assemblies with guest speakers and listened to musical presentations. Although there were no statues of him on campus, Whittier claimed Richard Nixon as one of its most famous graduates.

Autumns in LA were hot and dry, with the air often fouled by smog. It made running difficult, but I enjoyed the challenge. I was fortunate to have good teammates in Russ Bonham and Danny Schweikert, a 4:10-miler. Our friendship grew during our training runs on the roads around the college and during excursions to local beaches. We had cross-country meets almost every Saturday during the fall season. One of our meets was held at Big Bear at an elevation of six thousand feet. I had never run at high altitude before, and I paid a painful price. I now understand why the best distance runners train at least part of the year at nine-thousand-foot altitudes in order to stay competitive. Kenyans and Ethiopians have lived in the highlands of Africa for generations and have adapted to running in low-oxygen conditions.

Coach Bonham was happy with my running and my attitude. I improved upon all of my previous marks in the 880, mile, and two-mile during my first college track season. However, my one-year stay at Whittier College came to an end in 1954 for a couple of reasons. After a few months at the school, I realized that I was in the wrong major and knew that I would eventually have to change, which would mean a loss of time and money. Also, I learned that the GI Bill was going to be phased out after the end of the Korean War. Jim Fields, a friend from Seattle, suggested that we join the army in order to lock in GI Bill benefits when we returned to college.

ARMY LIFE (1954–56)

M y enlistment in the army was made less intimidating by the fact that Modris had already joined and was stationed in Germany during his two-year commitment. Jim and I were sent to Fort Ord, near the sandy, foggy shores of Monterey, for basic training. We had heard stories about the rigors that recruits must endure at the Hunter Liggett training grounds near Big Sur. Like all recruits, we had our heads shaved and our civilian identities discarded for six weeks. We took part in the American ritual of rising before dawn to be humiliated by a drill sergeant who keeps insisting that he loves you. I learned such valuable skills as shooting at people with an M-1 rifle while screaming at the top of my lungs. We learned to salute anyone who had more stripes than us (which was pretty much everyone), made messy kitchens spotless, acquired new and exciting swear words, and enjoyed the nighttime excitement of guard duty. To add insult to injury, everyone had to donate blood. The sergeant reminded recruits that were queasy about donating blood: "You don't own the blood; we do. Roll up your sleeve!" I can still picture my sergeant, who was an immigrant from the Philippines, and how frightened I was when he screamed at us for making stupid mistakes, which I seemed to do with regularity. Even when I saluted him, I was chewed out for carrying out an "unauthorized salute." I had forgotten that you weren't supposed to salute a lowly sergeant. Somehow, we survived and were rewarded with an impressive graduation parade. Whenever Joyce and I visit Carmel and the nearby sand dunes, it reminds me of the many times I fired my trusty M-1 rifle in those same dunes.

9. Atis "Pete" and Modris at the military
championships in Germany, 1956.

Thank God I was with Company A, since our destination after basic training was Germany. Those unfortunates in Company B were destined to spend the next two years freezing in South Korea. Germany, however, posed another danger. Soviet forces were conducting war maneuvers fifty to one hundred miles east of us. My company commander, Captain Burrer, had learned that I spoke some German, so he made me his jeep driver. He assumed that I would be able to ask locals for directions when we were lost (which was most of the time) or ordering food. It was better than carrying a rifle and pack through the snow and mud. Unfortunately, most of Europe was experiencing a brutal winter, which took all the fun out of our war games. Many of our scheduled maneuvers had to be cancelled because the jeep and truck engines froze up and soldiers suffered frostbite. The war would have to wait. During that dismal winter, the heater in the jeep saved me.

Captain Burrer was surprised that I was not yet an American citizen, and he asked me if I wanted to join my fellow soldiers as a US citizen. I had only resided in the United States for four years, so an opportunity to obtain citizenship so quickly was more than I had hoped for. Modris and I, along with other foreign-born soldiers, were escorted to US headquarters in Frankfurt. Army protocol is seldom carried out quickly and efficiently, so we were astounded when it only took thirty minutes to be sworn in and receive our citizenship documents. With a signature and raised hand, Modris and I became Americans. After that ceremony, we felt a new sense of pride when we put on our uniforms. Eventually, my parents and Jausma joined us in becoming citizens.

While playing soldier, I was able to continue running in order to participate in a camp track meet. I had retained some of my conditioning, and by winning a few preliminary races, I caught the attention of Captain Burrer, who was once a track-and-field athlete himself. He recommended me for a possible spot on the army's European team, which would be competing in the US military games in Los Angeles. The team candidates assembled in Nuremberg for additional training and trial competitions. The final trials would be held on the same parade grounds where Nazi rallies were held twelve years previously. It was a bittersweet reunion in Nuremberg; I was happy to compete for a spot on the all-army team, but I had unpleasant flashbacks to my years in the DP camps. It was surreal to think that we were running wind sprints in front of the graying stands where Hitler had smiled and saluted his hordes of marching soldiers.

After several wins in my qualifying races, I was chosen to compete in the mile run. Modris qualified in both 110-meter and 400-meter hurdle events. We knew we were fortunate for the opportunity to compete together on the same team. The army paid for our flight to Fort Roberts in San Pedro, California, where we would be stationed while we trained. We both looked forward to leaving army life behind for a month and returning to the United States. San Pedro is a working-class community overlooking Los Angeles Harbor and the city of Long Beach. It is the home of many Portuguese immigrants who work as fishermen. Fort Roberts was built on a bluff overlooking the Port of Los Angeles and Long Beach Harbor. It was a good place to overcome jet lag and reconnect with life in America. The military base had no track, so we held a few workouts at Long Beach City College, the site of the inter-service meet. Our training sessions gave us more confidence for the military games. We were excited about meeting athletes from the other branches of the service. None of us knew much about the backgrounds of our fellow competitors, but we did learn that the air force and the marines allowed athletes a half day off from military duties so they could be better prepared for the in-service rivalry. Modris and I knew we were in for tough races. I placed third behind two runners who had competed in college prior to enlisting for military service. By the end of the competition, I had less than four months left in my two-year commitment, so the army saw no need to send me back to Germany.

I was put on a military plane and flown to a base in Gig Harbor in Puget Sound, where I was discharged three months before my enlistment ended. Seeing the Puget Sound Islands from the base was a comforting sight. My duffle bag was packed with military gear that I hoped would never be used, and I arrived home to a warm reunion with my parents.

It was still summertime, which left me time to relax at home, compete in the Scottish Highland Games in Vancouver, and along with Modris and Bob Lawson, spend time fishing in Puget Sound. Bob, a decathlete from USC who had placed fourth in the Olympic trials, had grown up in Washington and returned to Seattle each summer.

At the end of the summer, Bob and I packed my VW bug and returned to Los Angeles. At Bob's suggestion, I enrolled at Los Angeles City College, a two-year community college. I was careful to enroll in classes that would be accepted for credit at a four-year school. It was a great suggestion, since I was able to enroll in classes taught by outstanding USC professors who happened to be moonlighting at City College. I never realized learning could be so exciting, and looked forward to my philosophy, American government, and anthropology classes. I also joined the LACC cross-country team. The semester flew by rapidly, and before I knew it, we were driving back to Seattle for Christmas.

While I was visiting my parents, I got a surprise call from Bob. He had talked to Jess Mortensen, the head track coach at USC, about my background as a distance runner. Evidently, Bob was persuasive, because Coach Mortensen offered me a USC track scholarship for the next three years. The opportunity to get a university education while competing on the USC track team was a life-changing event. The next time I saw Bob, he grabbed me by my shirt, nearly lifting me off the ground, and kiddingly challenged me: "Now don't you let me down." From that moment, I dedicated myself to do everything possible to justify his trust in me.

10. Atis "Pete" (far left) becoming a United States
citizen at the ceremony in Germany, 1956.

USC (1956-60)

realized that I was truly fortunate to have the opportunity to attend one our country's great private universities. The few classes I took at LACC from USC professors heightened my enthusiasm for what was yet to come. I looked forward to challenging classes and becoming part of a track program that had won so many NCAA titles. From the beginning, I knew I was with a select group of athletes and part of a program that had earned worldwide respect. My teammates included Olympians Max Truex, Charlie Dumas (the first high jumper over seven feet), and throwers Rink Babka and Dallas Long. Other outstanding Trojan athletes included Tom Anderson, Ted Smith, Bob Shankland, Wayne Lemons, Ted McCloud, and Maury Coburn from Canada. I had already met some of them while competing in the Scottish Highland Games during the summer. With such an impressive group of athletes, USC had yet to be beaten in a dual track meet. Ex-USC athletes Ron Morris, John Bragg, and Olympic champion Mike Larrabee took me under their wings and helped me assimilate into the impressive family of Trojan track athletes. Their confidence in me, and the expectations set by the USC track program, provided plenty of motivation. If my teammates were able to excel under the guidance of the USC coaches, then so could I.

11. U.S.C. teammates Bob Lawson and Pete, 1958.

My professors both inspired and challenged me. I was fascinated with the French Revolution covered in my European history class. Our professors presented us with the tools to make an informed analysis of US history, including questionable practices that had been omitted or overlooked by many of our former instructors. We learned new details about the Japanese internment during World War II, which had been approved by the US Supreme Court based upon a flimsy body of facts. Despite learning about some of the controversial practices during periods of our history, I came to admire the American political institutions.

Before enrolling at USC, I lacked confidence in public speaking; I was still afraid that I would make noticeable mistakes if I volunteered an answer in class. Of course, my lack of confidence carried over to relationships with the young ladies that I met. To overcome my shyness, I reluctantly signed up for speech, level one. My torturous pronunciations and shy stares at the floor while speaking amused my classmates. We were required to read a poem that was to be recorded, which would enable us to self-evaluate our speech. Two of my efforts included "Leonardo da Vinachi invented spinachi" and "The rain in Spain on the table makes a stain." That was the first time I had heard the sound of my own voice, and I was not impressed. I realized that my voice sounded different from how I thought it did. I also realized that the anxiety and lack of confidence during public speaking was shared by many of my classmates. We formed a bond in which we helped each other get through the stressful situations and came to understand that speech was a reflection of personal and societal values. The following semester I decided to continue to humble myself in speech, level two, with an additional class in phonetics. My efforts were rewarded because a new Pete emerged from each class. My speeches steadily improved, and my classmates were treated with fewer gaffes. I eventually ended up having enough units in speech to complete a minor.

My history professor found out that I was on the track team and would be running in a meet the following weekend. To my surprise, I noticed him sitting in the stands. After my race, I got up the nerve to ask him what he thought of my effort. With a sly smile, he replied, "You are a fair runner, but a much better history student." I took it as a compliment. I have kept and still treasure the essays that I wrote in his classes. My papers covered topics such as "The five people who had the greatest influence on the French Revolution" and "The encyclopedists and their role in shaping a modern and reasonable world." When I read them today, history once again comes alive.

My roommate at USC was Max Truex, who would become the best long-distance runner in USC history. Max came to USC from tiny, rural Warsaw, Indiana, and was understandably lost in sprawling Los Angeles. My good friend and former teammate, John Bragg, describes Max's first look at the USC campus: "When Max arrived in LA, Head Coach "Mort" Mortensen asked me, Mike Larrabee, and Lanny Quigley to take the tiny (five-foot-six) distance runner from Warsaw, Indiana, on a tour of campus and the surrounding area, including UCLA. Football teams were getting ready, and track meets would come shortly. Max had never seen the ocean, and probably had never ventured away from his hometown, so we took him to the beach at Santa Monica. On the way, we picked up some high-school girls at a bus stop. After dropping them off, we took him to the red-light district in downtown LA. To say the least, this innocent high-school runner, despite his reputation as a star, was overcome by the experience. The next morning, Coach Mort called us into his office, where we were unambiguously scolded for introducing Max to the steamy side of life in Los Angeles. Our coach, however, had nothing to worry about, because Max was the most honest and positively focused person I had ever met. Apparently, nothing fazed him, which helped explain the drive that made him a remarkable athlete and lawyer.

Finding a place to live at USC was difficult, so I persuaded Max to help me find an apartment. We found a fabulous place near school, on the second floor of a run-down building known as "The Jungle," so-called because of its inner courtyard festooned with trees and shrubs. I found out that all the houses on Twenty-Eighth Street were in the same decrepit condition but nevertheless filled with students. To make our house the one truly authentic jungle, we filled it with the sounds of Tarzan yells. Max was an outstanding student as well as one of the top distance runners in the United States. He finished sixth in the Rome Olympics at 10,000 meters. Max was also known for having a voracious sweet tooth. He seldom passed on an opportunity buy and consume prodigious amounts of cake and ice cream during study breaks. To ease his conscience, he always shared scraps of his bounty with me.

12. U.S.C. roommates Pete and Olympian Max Truex, 1957.

Max and I were introduced to the new distance coach, Dr. Jim Slosson, a professor of geology at Valley College and a USC graduate. "Dr. Jim" was instrumental in our group's improvement. He made use of many new and unusual techniques to teach running. Instead of always running mind-numbing repetitions on a track, he designed workouts to be run on the grass that surrounded the Coliseum, the iconic site of the 1932 and 1984 Olympics and the Trojan football stadium. We ran some workouts on roads and sometimes traveled to nearby beaches. He encouraged us to experiment with "fartlek," the "speed play" that had been popularized by the best Scandinavian distance runners. He was a father figure and good friend to our group, often letting us go on long runs or ride horses on his ranch. After our workouts, he treated us to barbecued steaks and ice cream, which made Max ecstatic. Dr. Slosson and his wife Nancy became our parents away from home, and they were instrumental in helping contribute to the significant improvement in our track times. Coach Mortensen was impressed and soon gave Dr. Slosson full control of the Trojan distance crew, including the rare privilege of allowing us choose which events we wanted to run in meets.

After a long illness, Max Truex died in 1991, leaving us at USC and the entire Los Angeles track community saddened. He had run the famous seven-mile "Midnight Race" in Rio de Janeiro. He led most of the race, but was forced to inhale dangerous concentrations of carbon monoxide from the motorcycles that guided the runners. The United States versus Soviet Union track meet was held in Philadelphia in near-one-hundred-degree heat and high humidity. After his 10,000-meter race, Max became so exhausted and dehydrated that he passed out. Doctors believe such extreme punishment to his body and brain lead to his premature death. Losing Max was a blow to all of us. Having earned a master's degree in accounting, he found it to be a monotonous career. He quit his job and enrolled in law school. He passed the bar exam, and for a short time, worked in the district attorney's office. Since Max was only five foot six, his friends thought about getting him a stool that he could stand on while arguing cases before a judge. I will be forever grateful to Max, who earned straight As, for helping me become a serious student and a more competitive runner. He was a valued friend.

My confidence as both a student and an athlete grew during my first year at USC. I ran lifetime bests in the 880, mile, two-mile, and 5,000-meter run. My one big win came against UCLA in the two-mile. The popularity of track and field was at an all-time high, with dual meets often attracting ten thousand spectators. Meets that specialized in relay races were fun for both spectators and athletes. I enjoyed being part of several record-setting teams at the Modesto, West Coast (Fresno), Coliseum, Compton, and Mount SAC Relays. Today, dual meets between university teams are rare, but we were always excited for our meets against Stanford, UCLA, Cal, Oregon, and Occidental. Our coaches also scheduled dual meets against the best club teams in California. In our meet against the Southern California Striders, the defending National AAU champions, USC defeated an elite Strider team that included Olympic champion Mike Larrabee in the last event of the meet, the mile relay (today called the 4x440). The thrilling relay win kept USC's twenty-year, eighty-win unbeaten streak intact. In the USC/Stanford/Oregon tri-meet in 1958, I noticed an Oregon runner by the name of Phil Knight, who was listed to run the mile race against Bob Shankland and me. I heard that he was a fairly good runner, but I never got the chance to race him, since he pulled out of the mile to run the 880. Many years later, I got a chance to know him during the summers while I was working for Nike. But we never had the opportunity to discuss the Stanford mile. I loved competing in front of standing-room only crowds in the beautiful tree-lined stadium of nearby Occidental College. The green enclosure made the Oxy track seem shorter than our home track in the cavernous Coliseum. Even today, I still exchange pictures and trade stories with my Oxy friend Hal Harkness. My teammates, who contributed so much with their individual support, made my experiences rich and rewarding. I am happy to have earned letters for my three years at USC, and I like to think that I justified Bob Lawson's decision to convince Coach Mortensen to take a chance on an unknown refugee from Latvia.

13. Pete winning the two-mile race in the dual meet with UCLA, 1959.

A NEW START AS A COACH (1959)

I stayed at USC for another year in order to get my teaching credential. My student-teaching assignment was at a local middle school, with a very stern and unhappy master teacher. He never smiled, and he reprimanded me when I projected a friendly disposition toward my students. He ordered me to lecture for most of the period and discouraged too many follow-up questions. Most importantly, he continued to emphasize that student's need strict discipline, which could dissolve if they caught you smiling. It was not a pleasant introduction to teaching. I learned little, and as a result of my experience, decided that an unnaturally stern approach would be both counterproductive and unpleasant for both my students and myself. I would always attempt to be myself: I liked kids and always tried to be friendly and respectful. There had to be a better way, one that promoted an enthusiastic environment for learning.

Although I had already graduated, it was still exciting to be at USC and have a chance to follow my former teammates and the new members of our track team. One day, I drove to Glendale to visit my dentist, who was also a USC graduate. I decided to stop by the track at Glendale Junior College, just to watch the distance runners going through interval sessions. The head coach, who was familiar with my background, let me know that he needed a distance coach. He asked me if I would agree to help coach their runners. I didn't know it at the time, but my chance encounter with the Glendale coach was a defining moment in my life: I made the change from competitive athlete to coach. It was the beginning of a thirty-year love affair with coaching. I decided at that point that one of my primary goals would be to instill the joy of running that I had experienced during the past decade in my athletes. "Run for Fun" would be a theme that defined my attitude toward our sport.

One of my first runners was Pat Connelly, who readily accepted my somewhat unconventional approach to distance running and enjoyed our training sessions. Years later, Pat became an officer in the LAPD, as well as a successful high-school coach. He organized the L.A. police-academy team, and assisted both UCLA and USC women's running programs. He has written numerous books on running and has enjoyed success as a motivational speaker.

A TEACHER (1960)

1960 was a pivotal year for recruiting out-of-state teachers for California schools. Southern California was experiencing extraordinary growth, and school districts couldn't build schools fast enough to keep up with the baby boomers that were packing into the existing buildings. In order to fill the ever-increasing need for quality instructors, many talented, creative, and engaging teachers were recruited from around the country. With my newly minted teaching credential from the state of California, I looked forward to beginning a new career. The Los Angeles Unified School District had an opening for a social studies teacher at Hughes Junior High School in Woodland Hills, which was nestled into a growing suburb of the San Fernando Valley. I was hired and warmly welcomed by a youthful faculty, many of them new teachers like myself. Woodland Hills was a newer community, and it was known for parents enthusiastically supporting their public schools. With so many fresh and creative educators, it didn't take long for me to feel at home. It was an ideal setting in which to begin a career.

Our staff often got together on weekends for barbecues, pool parties, and bowling. One day I noticed a fellow teacher hurrying from room to room with a large ring of keys around his neck. Martin Levine was also a newly hired member of our social studies department, and we formed an immediate bond. He had graduated from Bowdoin College in Maine, so he brought an East Coast ethic to our collection of mostly California-raised colleagues. Every time I walked by his room, I heard lively discussions, laughter, and a "life-in-the-classroom" atmosphere, where students were fully involved in the learning process. I seldom saw students sitting numbly in their seats and taking notes. My friendship with Marty turned out to be a blessing. His enthusiasm for his subject was infectious, for both his students and me. He utilized a variety of audiovisual materials that made simple stories come to life. He loved to include examples from the lives of common people as well as the better-known kings, philosophers, and inventors. His goal was to foster understanding of the entire civilization being studied instead of concentrating on isolated facts. I'll always remember Jules Mandel, our school's French teacher, who I invited to my class to teach the students *La Marseillaise* as a part of our unit on the French Revolution. He was dynamic, expressive, and managed to hold my students spellbound for a period, at the end of which they had learned the words and could sing France's national anthem in French. His lesson was so effective that I can still sing *La Marseillaise* in the original language. Teachers like Marty and Jules created a stimulating environment that made it easy for me to develop my own teaching style, one that liberated me from dependence on the traditional lecture form.

I couldn't help but notice our new vocal music teacher, Joyce Englestad, who had graduated from cross-town rival, UCLA. She became a popular teacher who motivated her students to take pride in their many and varied productions. There was an immediate mutual attraction between us, and I tried to figure out the best ways to get to know her better. I offered to photograph her choir performances, the results of which I insisted on delivering personally. She was appreciative, which made it easy for us to get better acquainted during our lunch breaks. We always sat across from each other in the lunchroom. One thing led to another as we became more comfortable in each other's presence, and we perfected a game of "footsies" under the table while exchanging romantic glances. Our first date was a drive to Malibu, where we enjoyed listening to the waves. After a few minutes, the magic of the water took over, and we embraced and kissed. Three years later, we were engaged to be married.

While Joyce and I were developing a serious relationship, a slim, blond language teacher named Karin joined our staff. Marty and Karin started dating and were married in 1964, the same year that Joyce and I were wed in a small chapel in North Hollywood. We were married on June 21 with my sister Jausma, her husband, Bob, Marty, Karin, and a few other friends in attendance. Marty, Karin, Joyce, and I have remained the best of friends ever since our teaching days at Hughes. We celebrated our fiftieth wedding anniversaries in the summer of 2014.

14. Wedding day for Pete and Joyce, June 1964.

TWO ROOKIE TEACHERS,
by Marty Levine, Thousand Oaks, California

In the late 1950s, I met "Trackman" Pete, who was a fellow social studies teacher at Hughes Junior High in Woodland Hills, California. We quickly became great friends. He served as best man at my wedding, and we now boast a special friendship that has lasted over fifty years. I once asked a twelve-year-old student at the junior high school who his favorite teacher was, and he replied, "Mr. Pete is my favorite teacher."

"What class do you have him for?" I continued. "I don't have him for any class," he answered. "But he's still my favorite teacher."

I heard that response more than once, and it illustrates just what a special person Pete is. I can't tell you how many of my own social studies students were bold enough to tell me that the previous year they had a "real" social studies teacher, Mr. Pete. It was bad for my ego, but it motivated me to do better. That's what makes Pete special: he motivates you to do better if you are a student, teacher, or runner.

15. Great friends and teaching colleagues, from left;
Martin & Karin Levine, Joyce & Pete, 2014.

PIERCE JUNIOR COLLEGE (1961)

Pierce Junior College was a sprawling community college that occupied the hills across the street from our school. The space was needed for the college to support its widely respected agricultural curriculum. It also offered traditional freshman and sophomore college courses, as well as an athletic program. Because of its agricultural roots, its athletic teams were called the Brahmas.

I, of course, was interested in their track-and-field program. I had seen their distance runners striding along the trails that wound through the campus, so I was itching to meet the coach and watch a training session. The Pierce coach, Bob Chambers, was a medalist in the 800-meter in the Helsinki Olympics and a USC grad. Like the Glendale coach, he also wanted to add a coach who could help with the distance runners and free up more time for him to work with sprinters and hurdlers. Coach Chambers felt that my coaching experience at Glendale and my running background at USC would meet the qualifications he needed for a new assistant coach. He asked me if I wanted the job, and I immediately accepted. Although I would receive no salary, the position would give me valuable experience and enable me to join the Pierce runners on some of their training runs. At that time, I was still trying to run on my own with the hope of getting into good enough condition to enter a race or two. Having a group of built-in training partners would make it easier to get into shape.

Pat Connelly had transferred from Glendale to Pierce, and although he had used up his eligibility, he was often on campus to run or to help Coach Chambers. Pat introduced me to my first Run for Fun group, which, although small, consisted of local runners who were open to trying out my somewhat unconventional training methods. Pat had recruited Dick Weeks and Preston Massey from Birmingham, his former high school, and Lew Barnett from Reseda High School, who was one of the best half-milers in the area. After Dick won the Southern California Junior College two-mile and Lew continued to improve as a middle-distance runner, word got out among local high-school runners that something unique was happening at Pierce.

The following year, the group grew considerably, with some of the best runners in the area deciding to join us. John Kennedy was a 4:20-miler from Verdugo Hills who eventually improved to 4:05, Martin Cooley attended high school in Taft, near Bakersfield, and Jim Backus, although quiet and reserved, turned out to be a tenacious competitor. Bill Scobey and Bill Berridge from Cleveland High School, Jay Romais from Taft, and Al Shank from Canoga Park all thrived in our Run for Fun environment. The Pierce cross-country team went from the bottom of the conference to champions in one year. Since distance runners were not the only ones allowed to enjoy running, we were joined by sprinters Rich Achee, Dennis Chinaieff, and Al Bennett, who enabled the Brahma track team to continue the success enjoyed by the cross-country team. Our accomplishments, achieved in only two years, became the envy of other junior college programs.

I was still a novice as a coach, but after experiencing such enjoyable years as a track athlete at USC, I felt that I had a foundation around which a competitive program could be built. Runners yearn for an intelligent, innovative, and enjoyable experience. My goal as a coach at Pierce was to provide training sessions that utilized a variety of techniques. We encouraged the runners to have fun during our sessions: run relaxed and don't stress over the stopwatch, don't be afraid to vary the speed and distance of the training runs, and don't lock yourself into the attitude that a track is the only place to train. Dick Weeks reminded me that he knew things were going to be different when he saw me walking up from the grass fields on the lower part of campus with a gasoline can in my hand. I had used the gasoline to burn a 440-yard track into the grass in order to provide my runners with another surface to enjoy. They could all be kids again.

Running on grass was just one of the innovations that I tried. The runners soon learned that our loosely structured wind sprints would be referred to as "shakeups," a term borrowed from László Tábori. The rolling hills of Pierce provided an ideal setting to practice "fartlek" runs, which allowed runners to be creative in an attempt to vary the length and tempo of the session. They joined in games of "running golf" by striding between the greens on the Sepulveda Basin golf course. We bodysurfed at Zuma Beach and played Frisbee or touch football during our warm-up sessions. The athletes never knew what to expect from day to day, but that just added to the fun. We avoided getting into a rut, and the runners learned to become comfortable and relaxed while running with a short stride, long stride, fast pace, or easy pace. There was no guarantee that our system would create champions, but as I saw the runners showing steady improvement, I was inspired to continue innovating.

I had faith in what I was doing as a coach. I was free to adapt and innovate, often as a response to feedback from my runners. Borrowing from my teaching of the Buddhist monk's power of concentration in my World History classes, I started stressing the quality of running as softly as possible, without making the sound of landing on the feet, like falling leaves to the ground, making barely a sound. Often I covered my eyes, listening to my runners passing by me to judge their improvement.

David Epstein writes in his excellent book, *Sports Gene*, describing one of our great marathon runners Tony Sandoval, "There was no wasted movement in his stride, he seems to barely come off the ground, sweeping over the soil as light as a water bug flitting on the pond." I remember seeing Tony run the 5000m race in Oslo, Norway, coming away highly impressed with his smooth, effortless stride.

Gerry Lindgren, who I worked with at Lake Tahoe in 1968, told me, "Running should be an adventure, instead of only a workout." Since I was still running in the early sixties and entering some all-comers meets, I could illustrate striding techniques and join my runners in parts of their workout sessions. Bill Scobey recently remarked that I would pace runners through 880 yards in time trials at a two-minute pace and manage to look relaxed doing it. He commented, "Pete sure runs smoothly for an old man!" None of my runners had ever had a coach join them in workouts. They realized that I wouldn't put them through anything that I couldn't do myself, which gave me an extra level of credibility. I believe much of our success was a result of our group camaraderie; the athletes were able to share their joy of running with others. Other coaches, along with newspapers, *Runner's World* magazine, and Track and Field News took notice of our success in the Southern California and State JC Championship meets. Our little agricultural college in the San Fernando Valley had become a distance running powerhouse.

PETE AND THE RUNNING MONKS,
by Dick Weeks, Eugene, Oregon

Martin, John, and I were members of Pete's original group of Run for Fun athletes at Pierce College in 1962. At twenty-eight, Pete was only about ten years older than most of his runners. He was unlike any coach we had known before. Most of our previous coaches had been football players who knew little about the requirements of running any distance longer than one hundred yards. They embraced the PTA (Pain, Torture, and Agony) philosophy of generations of frustrated football coaches who were forced to deal with the gaunt distance runners under their supervision. Pete was an ex-USC distance runner and a former roommate of Max Truex, an Olympian and one of America's legendary track athletes. With his Latvian roots, Pete was strongly influenced by European athletic philosophy and techniques. He introduced the element of "play" into our training regimen: we ran barefoot on grass instead of endless circles around a cinder track. We shared jokes and had contests to determine who could come closest to imitating the running style of Emil Zátopek, the famous Czech Olympian. Under Pete's guidance, running became a consistent source of joy and excitement in our lives. It had to, because the wild college social scene that we envisioned had completely eluded us. All we did was study and run: we were running monks.

Our workout sessions became an outlet to air our frustrations. John and Martin, with their type-A personalities, talked as fast as they ran. John would complain about how out of shape he was by reciting a catalog of muscles and joints that were sore. Martin's topic of choice for complaints was city girls. He grew up in Taft, a small town about one hundred miles north of Los Angeles, where, he insisted, good-looking ladies waited in line for him to ask them out. With little coaxing, Martin would produce an old, creased photo of Jamie, his hometown girlfriend.

"Jamie isn't stuck up like all the L.A. girls," he proclaimed.

Pete became the calming influence that kept our group in a state of semi-cohesiveness. As someone who dated women during this time, he was seen as a reliable source for how we might escape a sentence of perpetual geekiness. On one Friday afternoon, we had just finished a long workout and were doing a warm-down jog when Pete suggested that the four of us see *The Loneliness of the Long-Distance Runner*. Although Martin, John, and I knew nothing about the movie, we could readily identify with the title. The film was playing in a small "art-house" theater in Hollywood, so we piled into Pete's '57 VW bug and drove "over the hill" to Sunset Boulevard. We expected to see an inspiring story about the nobility and determination needed to run long distances. But instead we saw a dark and brooding film about the prison experience of a petty criminal who happened to be a talented runner. Pete enjoyed the movie, but the rest of us failed to recognize the criticism of the British class system woven into the story. All we understood was that the prisoner quit a race he was leading just to wreak revenge on the warden.

On the drive home, we suspected the foreboding movie had put Martin into a foul mood. As usual, he vented his frustration by complaining about L.A. girls. After several minutes of listening to his staccato ramble about the difficulties of meeting local women, Pete decided to make a move that had the potential to shut Martin up for a long time. We were on the 405 Freeway doing about fifty-five miles per hour, close to top speed for the little VW, when Pete pulled even with a car occupied by four young girls. Before we realized what was happening, he rolled down his window and made circular motions with his hand to signal to the attractive girls in the target car to do the same. Martin quit talking, and a tense silence fell over our cramped quarters. We could see the girls giggling as they rolled down their windows. Pete yelled out, "Follow us to DuPar's!" One of the girls yelled something back, which we couldn't hear, but we concluded that it wasn't, "Get lost."

We pulled ahead of the car, turned around in our seats, and watched in astonishment as the girls slowed and merged into our lane. Within a few minutes, we were pulling into the parking lot at DuPar's, a popular restaurant in Sherman Oaks, with the ladies right behind.

The four young women were as friendly as they were attractive. We ordered ice cream for all and talked about movies, school, and possible mutual friends. They were still in high school, and as we could see, they were also quite proud of themselves for being so daring as to accept a meeting with strange men, arranged while speeding along a crowded L.A. freeway. Martin managed a strained smile but added little to the conversation. John tried to compensate for Martin's uncharacteristic silence by talking incessantly. The girls looked at each other, trying patiently to make sense of what was being said. Before the situation deteriorated irreversibly, Pete redirected the conversation back to movies—something we could all understand. We finished our ice cream and said good-bye, still laughing about the improbability of this evening ever being repeated. Pete's ingenious plan to dispel the myth of the stuck-up city girl proved successful: Martin never brought up the subject again.

The spontaneous rendezvous in the restaurant elevated Pete to near-godlike status. We never managed to get up enough courage to duplicate the event, but it didn't matter. Pete had shown us that anything was possible. We realized that our pitiful state of social isolation was entirely self-imposed.

John, Martin, and I would soon complete our season at Pierce and move on to the university level. We were enriched by the Run for Fun experience with our new coach, fully aware that the fun didn't begin or end on the track. Pete's teachings were profound, lasting, and worthy of being passed on to a new generation of athletes.

Eventually, we attracted other runners, including Dean Smith, a former Texas sprinter who wanted to keep in shape for his roles in westerns as a double stunt man for Dale Robertson. Bob Day, Gene Comroe, and Dick Weeks joined our group after graduating from UCLA. The running grapevine extended beyond Southern

California, and our training group welcomed Ricardo (Rich) Romo from Texas and Ted Nelson from Mankato State in Minnesota. Ricardo, who was eager to become the first Texan to break the four-minute barrier in the mile, and Ted thrived under our system. Both Rich and Ted succeeded in running under four minutes, but Rich's running career was cut short by injuries. Rich, although slowed on the track, enthusiastically embraced his academic pursuits. He earned his doctorate in Mexican-American studies at UCLA and authored an acclaimed history of East Los Angeles. He now heads the University of Texas at San Antonio and has been awarded the prestigious Basilica de España for his contribution to Spanish culture.

All of the local and out-of-state runners took advantage of my association with the Southern California Striders track club, which provided a convenient outlet for ex-college runners to continue their participation in the sport. Ted, John Kennedy, Jay Romais, and Bill Scobey became firefighters, while Pat Connelly started innovative running programs for the LAPD. With the Vietnam War dragging on, Martin Cooley joined the army. It was rewarding to see several of my runners become successful high-school and club coaches, continuing to spread our Run for Fun philosophy to a new generation of athletes. The connection that was built with so many athletes has lasted for decades, and we still manage to stay in touch. These were part of the fun years, the years during which Joyce and I were able to form lasting bonds with a joyous, fun-loving group of people. Just last year (2014), many of our athletes and their wives reacquainted at a reunion at The Landing on the beautiful Westlake lake.

RUN FOR FUN

My philosophy of running began on our farm in Latvia. It was the ideal setting in which to experience the freedom and joy of movement. For as long as I can remember, I viewed running as a natural way to connect to the beauty of my surroundings. I loved striding along the trails, woods, hills, and pastures of the country-side around our home. The idea of running as an uplifting and liber-ating form of expression is a unifying theme in my involvement with the sport of track and field.

To call me a coach may be an overstatement, since I consider myself more of an advisor, friend, or even a conscience of the ath-letes that I deal with. Even though athletes have communicated to me their faith in what I attempted to accomplish, I see coaching as an extension of teaching, my profession for fifty years. I use some of the same techniques to motivate athletes as I do the high-school students in my history classes. A common thread in the process of motivating both history students and 1,500-meter runners is the ability for each individual to experience the fun that is involved in the endeavor.

"Run for fun, and from the fun will come the will to succeed." I al-ways felt that running was an enjoyable activity, and one of my primary goals was to communicate that attitude to my athletes. I wanted to produce confident, conscientious, and independent runners who were secure in the knowledge that they were capable of discovering their own potential. I make a point of encouraging athletes to start thinking and making decisions for themselves as soon as they join our training group. I remind athletes that, after leaving our group, they should be able to figure out the best training program for themselves or other athletes. If they can't, then I haven't done my job.

My joy comes from seeing an athlete blossom into a champion or observing an individual who develops the self-awareness to discover the keys to success. I watched Bill Toomey transform himself from a somewhat insecure, itinerant athlete into a confident champion. I assumed the role of catalyst. He had confidence that I could help both inspire and, at times, coddle him as he trained to be a world-class decathlete. I tried to achieve the balance between pointing out mistakes and reinforcing natural talents. Everything we achieved was designed around meshing his training with his unique learning style and, in the end, assuring him that he was on the right track.

I have never imposed my philosophy on any athlete. I don't believe in recruiting athletes by promising that I will transform them into champions. Athletes usually came to me, and I only worked with those who were willing to engage in a training program at a mature level. We avoided what came to be known as PTA workouts (pain, torture, and agony) that emphasized time over quality of effort. I have observed many coaches putting athletes through workouts that are delineated by time (e.g., twenty times 400 meters in sixty seconds). These workouts often leave athletes frustrated if they cannot run each quarter mile in sixty seconds or less, since success is measured by the stopwatch. I feel that the runner's ability to use proper form and run relaxed is more important than time.

I learned valuable training techniques from my friend, Coach Bud Winter of San Jose State. His runners were famous for having efficient form, which produced a swift carryover of speed. I watched him illustrate two techniques in a sprinting clinic in Venezuela. He told runners to run the first sprint as fast as they could—an all-out effort. He timed the runners. In the second sprint, he told the runners to run with proper form, concentrating on relaxation and avoiding strain. To their surprise, the runners recorded faster times in the second sprint.

The Elements of Run for Fun:

1. Variety

    - Vary the locale: track, grass fields, trails, beach sand, hills
    - Vary the speed
    - Vary the distance: avoid running the same distance during the entire workout (e.g., twenty times 400 meters). Instead, break up the workout into a variety of distances (e.g., seven times 200 meters, two times 800 meters, seven times 300 meters)
    - Vary the effort: endurance is gained by the combination of hard anaerobic runs balanced by easier aerobic sessions
    - Vary the stride length: a runner should be aware of when a shorter, quicker stride is more useful than a longer stride with greater hip rotation

2. Run efficiently: concentrate on form and relaxation over speed
3. Run for fun: running is a source of joy and fulfillment—don't spoil it

One day I got the idea of making up a Run for Fun T-shirt that I could give my Pierce runners as a reward and to symbolize the approach we took to training. Although I can't remember the exact date of production of the first batch of shirts, it served as a tangible statement of why we existed as a group. The T-shirt experiment surprised me when so many athletes wanted to wear one. After that point, and several batches of shirts later, we saw runners from all over the country wearing Run for Fun on their chests. Gary Tuttle recently located his faded relic of a Run for Fun shirt and displayed it on Facebook. It was captioned "Memories are made of this."

I fell in love with these first Run for Fun groups and consider my association with them as a highlight of my coaching career.

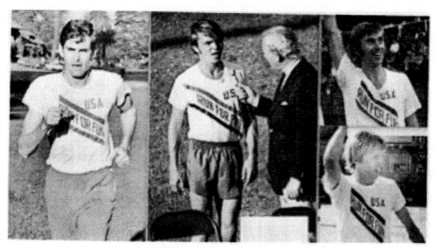

16. Run for Fun; from left, Jim Ryun, Steve Prefontaine, Arne Kvalheim and Tom Farrell..

FAST TRACKS, by Bill Scobey, San Luis Obispo, California

The mentorship I received from Atis "Pete" Petersons was the biggest reason for my success as a distance runner. His charismatic personality and Run for Fun ethos permeated every aspect of his coaching. The mundane mechanics of running (stride length, relaxation, and race tactics) took on a new meaning under Pete's guidance. He taught me to "leech" (draft off of another runner) and suggested subtle ways to "get into the head" of my opponents. His teaching was a major reason why I developed such a passion for the sport and was able to keep going for so long: logging more than 150,000 miles in my career. I learned much from Pete in a short period of time.

One of my favorite memories of Pete was the methodical manner in which he would prepare the old, beat-up clay track at the Pierce College stadium. One afternoon during the spring of 1963, I showed up at the track early for a workout and found a fit, twenty-nine-year-old Pete in his white Southern California Striders silk running shorts—his tanned muscles shining with perspiration as he meticulously worked the track surface with a push broom. Pete explained to me that all the fast tracks (Fresno, Modesto) were systematically prepared by hand in the same way he was demonstrating. This was well before the early synthetic tracks of South Lake Tahoe, Oregon, and Mexico City of 1968.

I watched in awe as Pete watered down the gravel surface before tying a rope to the rear bumper of his Volkswagen bug. He tied the rope to a section of chain-link fence and drove laps around the track oval—grating the surface to a perfect smoothness. After another watering of the newly groomed surface, he used a push broom to sweep the loose gravel into piles. He then shoveled the piles into a wheelbarrow and deposited them along the hillside surrounding the track. He repeated the process, taking extra care on the long sprint straightaways until he had the perfect clay surface. After grooming the surface to a condition that he was satisfied with, he would summon the school maintenance crew, which would then chalk the lane lines, starting lines, stagger marks, and passing zones. Pete would spend the entire track season repeating the ritual grooming process: the results of which earned Pierce the reputation as one of the premier tracks in the L.A. area.

Pete's dedication and tedious attention to detail produced a work of art framed into a perfect bowl-like stadium, protected from winds and surrounded by rolling chalk hillsides: a perfect setting for fast times and memorable competitions. To complete the setting, cross-country races were held in the hills above the stadium. Since the mid-1950s, the Pierce cross-country course would become the site of all Los Angeles city high school cross-country and several AAU championship races.

The summer of 1964 was a banner year for Pete's lovingly groomed oval. Bob Schul, paced by some of his Los Angeles Track Club teammates, set a new world record for the two-mile run (8:26.4). At another Pierce College summer meet the same year, Ricardo Romo from Texas and Ted Nelson from Minnesota paced each other to their first and only sub-four-minute miles, to date the only ones ever run on the Pierce track. The following year members of the Pierce College distance team set the national junior college record in the 4x1-mile relay. As Pete and I parted, he wrote out a series of five interval track workouts on a little slip of paper, which I kept in my wallet for more than thirty years. This paper became the basis for my personal speed-work sessions and for my years of coaching distance runners. I still have this worn slip of paper glued to a special page in a scrapbook that my mother started for me while I was in high school. Some memories never fade. I am so proud and thankful to have had Pete and Joyce in my life for over fifty years.

17. Rich Romo (3.58.6) and Ted Nelson (3.59.2) break 4
minute mile at 1964 Pierce All-Comers' meet, 1966.

SANTA BARBARA (1965)

The success we enjoyed with the Pierce College distance runners created new opportunities. Sam Adams, the track coach at the University of California, Santa Barbara, offered me a one-year position as the coach of the cross-country team. His offer was tempting, but I was hesitant to leave my highly-enjoyable teaching job of five years at Hughes Middle School, and as a Pierce College part-time running coach where I experienced my first coaching opportunity with the finest young college runners. But Joyce and I could not resist moving to this beautiful city famous for its beauty and world-class climate. So we rented a small apartment and gathered our belongings, including Joyce's grand piano, and started our new university-centered life. As a member of the UCSB faculty, my other assignments besides coaching distance runners was teaching a women's volleyball class and a class of well-skilled soccer players. Both classes were already adept and knew more than I did about their sport, so I joined a golf class next to our field and I learned how to play golf.

Once again, I was blessed with a group of outstanding individuals who were also accomplished students typically enrolled in challenging academic programs. Although most of our athletes were not highly recruited in high school, they were serious runners and enjoyed our training sessions. We had a successful cross-country season. While at Santa Barbara, I met Bill Toomey, who had graduated from the University of Colorado. I was happy to work with such an outstanding personality and talented athlete.

BILL TOOMEY

When I first met Bill, he certainly didn't look like a gold medal winner and record holder in the decathlon. His face was ashen, he was emaciated and fatigued, and he looked like someone who had lost too much weight. Bill thought he was just getting over a bout of mononucleosis, but it was more serious, he had contracted hepatitis while training in Germany, followed by six months recovery in a hospital, arriving in Santa Barbara in a weakened state. He had also previously shattered his kneecap in a car accident. But perhaps the most serious injury occurred to him at an earlier age. He explained to me, "When I was twelve, I was a victim of a pretty stupid trick. A kid threw a dish and it tore into my wrist. The nerve was severed in half". An accident such as this cut could put an end to his athletic dreams, since it involved the shot put, pole vault, discus and javelin throw. Doctors gave him little hope. It was a miracle that he was able to overcome the loss of strength in his right wrist and still succeed beyond expectations. Years later, Bill felt "The greatest feeling of accomplishment for me is the fact that I was an athlete who was able to accomplish so much while being somewhat disabled." Bill tried to keep this secret for as long as possible from his opponents.

These setbacks didn't deter his plans. He had already gone through a rough period after finishing fourth in the previous U.S. Olympic Trials in 1964, losing a spot on the USA team by a mere 109 points. But he seemed determined to gain his strength back and regain his form no matter what, so that he could continue his quest for a spot on the 1968 Olympic team in Mexico City.

BEAUTIFUL SANTA BARBARA

Bill was a newcomer to Santa Barbara, figuring that the tranquil, ideal year-round climate would give him the best chance for a quick recovery. Having Coach Sam Adams, who was a former decathlete, helping him with the field events, certainly made it easy to become enthused. As he was recovering from his weakness, he asked me to help him to resume his training. I was happy to be able to work with such a dedicated athlete and impressed with his enthusiasm and gutsy attitude to start training all over again. Only the hardiest ones who love their sport and truly enjoy training have what it takes to overcome a lousy fourth place finish. I became convinced that he was no ordinary athlete. He liked training and the companionship of others, especially with his good friends, Barry King, an Englishman and fierce competitor and Russ Hodge, who was the world record holder and a participant in the 1964 Olympic Games in Munich. The three of them found a place, living like a couple of track-and-field monks just a short distance from the beautiful, eucalyptus-tree lined UCSB campus. They developed a friendship based on mutual trust and respect. Russ was an impressive, solidly-built 6'3", weighing 224 pounds, all-around athlete. We were all amazed that he could run 10.2 one hundred meters and throw the shot over 61 feet. His only problem was his constant injuries.

Coach Sam Adams and Bill had attracted other decathletes, including John Warkentin, Fred Dixon, Dave Thorson and Harry Marra, establishing a decathletes' mecca. Other decathletes from all over heard about the beautiful place and wanted to come to Santa Barbara, especially after Mexico City, mostly due to Bill's success and Coach Adams' help. Many came from Germany to train after hearing Bill tout the fine weather, beautiful city and beaches. Harry Marra was the shortest of our decathletes but the one with the most determination and biggest heart. He has since become an outstanding all-around coach. Harry now coaches Ashton Eaton, a gold medal and world record holder.

GETTING STARTED

It didn't take long for us to get started. Putting all of Bill's tragedies behind, but still feeling fatigued, Bill began his long climb toward recovery. He was a very unusual athlete with a keen intellect and a highly educated background. He had acquired a thirst for learning and mastering new areas, whether it was literature, politics or sports. With rare ability to remember everything he read and everybody that he met, he developed insights into new areas. All of a sudden there was excitement and fun added to our training. Like the regenerated and reborn Greek god of Phoenix, he obtained a new life by arising from ashes.

We also took notice of his influence around us. It didn't take us long to know this endearing newcomer. Within a short time he transformed our training environment with his intellect, humor and flashy personality. It felt like "Mr. Charisma" had arrived in Santa Barbara. He certainly didn't lack ideas. He was able to project original ways of thinking, doing things, whether discussing nutrition, sports, politics, education, movies or literature.

EARLY BEGINNINGS AS AN ATHLETE

While he was in high school and later at Worcester Academy in Massachusetts, he enjoyed playing many sports, including basketball. He was amazed how high he could jump for the rebounds and sail through the air. This led to a new event. He took up long jumping, which eventually earned him a track scholarship at the University of Colorado. Being unsure of which events to concentrate on, he tried as many as possible and enjoyed all of them. While still a youngster he loved jumping over barriers and over the home-made high jump stands.

By his own admission, he explained that during his early years he was far from being an outstanding athlete. He would say he was "mediocre" in everything he tried, but nevertheless, he continued to seek new ways to improve, to gain an edge. He knew that he had a long and arduous road ahead. Bill told me that he had his own "bag of tricks" theory on continuously seeking ways to improve. He said, "There is no big move you can make in training and competition, but there are thousands of little things you can do, and eventually reach perfection. If you add information and you are flexible, and always examine what you are set out to do, you'll be successful"

RUNNING WITH THE STRIDERS

Before coming to Santa Barbara he had already competed in the pentathlon, winning five U.S. titles. Still undecided about his best event, he took part in as many of them as possible. By joining the Southern California Striders, a new Bill was emerging. He loved running whenever there was a race, especially the relays with his talented Strider teammates. But he but also entered the long jump and hurdle events. He was beginning to enjoy the new challenging atmosphere in Southern California. He was no closer to deciding on his one event, but it didn't matter. He loved the fellowship of Mike Larrabee, John Pennel, Ron Whitney, Cliff Wily, Don Quarrie, and Geoff Vanderstock. We certainly didn't lack track meets during the late 1960's in California. There was a competition somewhere every weekend: Fresno Relays, Modesto Invitational, Bakersfield Invite, Coliseum Relays, Compton Relays and the Mt. Sac Relays. This gave Bill ample opportunities, including more pentathlons and decathlons.

His first Olympic Trial effort in 1964 resulted in a highly disappointing fourth place finish, which is by far the most agonizing result for any athlete seeking a spot on the team. Waiting four years seemed like a lifetime and the ever-present feelings of failing again questioned his choices. However, Bill became more than ever dedicated and convinced that he would land on the victory stand in

MALE TRACK ATHLETE OF THE YEAR

BILL TOOMEY

Mexico. In 1964, he was so intrigued with the decathlon that he paid his own way to see the Tokyo Olympic Games. It was there that he realized he had what it takes to improve in the field events, especially pole vault. He already possessed good speed for the 100m, 400m, long jump, all involving speed and strength. One of his early accomplishments of winning five straight US pentathlons practically became "his" event, he owned it, with nobody coming close to winning so many of them.

I had watched Bill run many races. As a member of my club, the Southern California Striders, he had ample meets in which to compete. The Striders were the best team in the country, an unusual group made up of athletes from all over the country and even foreigners who lived in the US. Jamaican Don Quarrie, a graduate of USC, he won the 200m race in Montreal Olympics in 1976, just to mention one. Our volunteer coaches like Chuck Coker, Jim Bush and me, along with volunteer doctors led by the gracious Dr. Harry Silver, who helped injured athletes, were most appreciated. In Mexico City, eighteen Striders made the team. Bill was one of them, as were Ron Whitney, John Pennel, Bob Day, Marty Liquori and other teammates.

BECOMING A NEW RUNNER: TRAINING WITH PETE

Bill had good speed but an awkward running form. I noticed his bad habits especially when running "all out". He seemed to be out of sink and it prevented him from achieving results that he was capable of. He reminded me of a runaway Mac truck, or a bull in a china shop crushing everything in his way. He seemed to be obsessed with winning, no matter what. Every time he stepped on the starting line, his competitors felt his fierce determination.

We agreed that emphasis of learning proper running form would provide a solid basis for his return to fitness. He tended to exert himself too much which made it difficult to concentrate on using efficient running form. He needed to slow down and sprint efficiently before he could unleash his typical go-for-broke running style. At times he looked like a windmill, with arms flailing and the veins in his neck revealing the strain of his effort and his head bobbing from side to side.

We engaged in interval sessions that stressed maximum relaxation, proper arm carriage and a gradual increase of speed. Bill was a fast learner who quickly understood how his new training methods would enable him to attain his goals.

Bill was an intelligent student and he quickly understood how his new training methods would enable him to attain his goals. He became confident and anxious to plan his own training sessions, but always discussing them with me to see my reaction. He mixed his weight training and field event days devoid entirely of running. The legs needed rest. Bill observed, "Very slowly, and with Pete's help, I climbed back to fitness. I found the effort I put into a session caused no discomfort, it seemed easy. In training, I didn't trash the body flat out, as I was used to. My training consisted of build-ups, starting with a reasonable pace, and then gradually speeding up over the last dozen yards progressively. That increase in speed is hardly noticeable during the work-out. I am able to train even when tired and yet without fatiguing myself. I do the same amount of work as I would any other way, and yet the quality of the faster portion is much better than I could manage if I went flat out all the way. I recover much more quickly too."

I served more as his "sounding board" and allowed him to choose his own training sessions, acting like his "conscience". This way he could include types of distances that he felt were needed. He showed remarkable progress in improvement with every session, running increasingly faster hundred to three hundred meter intervals, with a form that was relaxed and under control. How would he do under pressure demanding near all-out efforts? He certainly had improved in my favorite test run I designed for all of my runners. It was usually done at the end of our work-out, requiring him to run one 200 meter distance, at near-full effort, using a "swing" stride... but not all-out! Since the test run came at the end of the workout, I felt that they were able to run with most efficiency. I was surprised how quickly Bill improved his times and in such a short time. One big test came when the Olympic gold medal winner in the four hundred meters, Mike Larrabee, and Ron Whitney showed up for a time trial in the 300 meters that was supposed to be run with a near-maximum effort. All of them being competitive, it ended as an all-out effort with all three runners finishing together. He had passed my test. I knew he was ready for the Olympics. When Bill arrived in Santa Barbara, he was a 48.5 meter runner, while in the Mexico Olympics he set a new decathlon record of 400m in 45.6, the last event at the end of a twelve-hour decathlon competition. This was run very late in the evening, after a twelve-hour decathlon competition. Bill had lost so much of his liquids that it took him hours to be able to provide a urine sample required of all winners. He went on to win the gold medal. He also improved his 100-meter time from 10.5 seconds to 10.26 seconds and his long jump to 26'04" meters.

He wasn't finished yet. The year after the Olympics, in 1969 he set a new record, amassing 8417 points. It was set in the tenth decathlon of the year, a feat that would be comparable to a marathon runner competing practically every month of the year. Although his decathlon record has been broken a number of times, he played a major role in popularizing the event and putting it in sports headlines and making the decathlon one of the top prime events in the Olympics today. In August 2015, Ashton Eaton, under the coaching of Henry Marra, broke the 400m record that Bill held for 47 years!

I believe Bill had a "hate-love" relationship with the decathlon, enjoying winning twenty three of them out of thirty-three that he entered. He was so obsessed in completing all of them, no matter how injured he was in some of them. This surely must be a record by itself and more than likely will never be surpassed.

He maintained close ties with the German decathletes, Joachim Wolde and Kurt Bendelin, with whom he had the fiercest competitions, finishing second and third in Mexico. He believes the help he received from Friedl Shirmer, their famous German specialist in the weight events, while training with them in Germany helped him immensely to achieve maximum points possible. He has been invited back many times and received honors and reminisce their Olympic experiences.

Winning the Sullivan Award which is awarded to the best amateur athlete, was one of the most prized awards, since only a few decathletes had won it. In addition, Bill was also selected in 1968 as the ASBC's Athlete of the Year beating out all other professional athletes.

Following his triumph, Bill received many invitations to meet kings, presidents, and world leaders. In Ethiopia he received valuable ornaments, painted animal skins, art pieces, carvings and other treasures. While visiting Kenya, he brought with him a copy of ABC's Olympic coverage, which included many Kenyan runners winning many gold medals. They had not seen any of the Olympic coverage before. Bill told me that there was so much outburst of euphoria, people weeping uncontrollably, tears running down their cheeks. They saw their biggest hero, Kip Keino, beat Jim Ryun of U.S in the 1500 meters; Amos Bitwott in the steeplechase (he never got his shoes wet, since he cleared the area by jumping over it); and Naftali Temu winning the event most familiar to the Kenyans, the 10,000 meters.

On one such trip to Venezuela, he didn't have a gift for their president, so Bill presented his javelin. The president accepted it graciously even though it was a total surprise. Bill still has a picture of the president holding the javelin, with the wrong end up.

President Nixon chose him as the USA representative to the Munich Olympics. On a personal note, Joyce and I are forever grateful for Bill's efforts in securing me invitations as a guest coach for my assignments in Venezuela, Grenada and eventually Saudi Arabia. We were able to travel as a family and experience the lifestyles of the people we met.

Sportscasters and news reporters found Bill to be one of their favorite athletes to interview. He had become a charismatic figure who was never at a loss for words, providing quotes and views, offering unique viewpoints and personal experiences. Even years later, they knew Bill had an interesting, worthwhile comment on practically any topic.

~ On his success: "Perfection consists not so much in doing extraordinary things, but in doing ordinary things extraordinarily well."

~ About victory: "There is no one magic move or secret that creates victory, but lots of little items that are added together can make one victorious."

~ After his fourth- place finish in the '64 Trials he simply added," I gave it all, that's all you can do. Don't regret anything."

~ On the journey: "Realize that from the start every activity that comprises the journey has value and ability to teach you something."

~ On East German success, he explained, "The East Germans used biomechanics. This meant that rather than guessing about technique and form, they could apply changes to athletic performance based on science." This has carried over to today's German athletes, who excel in shot put, discus, and javelin throwing.

OUR FRIENDSHIP

Bill was more than an athlete who came into my life and with whom I worked, we became very close friends. We shared countless track meets, enjoyed many dinners, traveled together with CBS TV Sports Specials that were shown in Europe and the US. Bill insisted that I travel with him as his statistician.

Life became more exciting, especially in Santa Barbara, when Bill and his wife Mary bought a beautiful home in secluded Winchester Canyon. We enjoyed the times we shared with them and their two daughters, Samantha and Sarah, who were close to the same age as our daughter Marni. Even now that our girls have grown into adulthood, we all stay in touch!

MEMORIES WITH MARY

Mary is very close to our hearts. When we first met her, we instantly fell in love with her. Her personality captivated us with her genuine smile and her friendliness and her distinct and delightful British accent. She is a special lady indeed. It's no wonder that British people still consider her one of their most outstanding athletes. By winning the long jump gold medal, placing second in the pentathlon, and a bronze medal for the 4x100 meter relay in the Tokyo Olympics in 1964, no wonder her name has become synonymous with British excellence.

I found out just what a superior athlete she was when, shortly after the Olympics, she casually joined my runners in wind sprints. Her speed was still there when my runners could hardly stay up with her. Getting to know her as an athlete has also resulted in meeting her close friends. Through her we met Ron Pickering, Mary's coach and coach of the British team, and his wife Jean and son Shaun. Both Ron and Jean established a track scholarship fund for the British athletes that resulted in great progress for British athletes. We were invited to stay with them in their beautiful home that was surrounded by fragrant flowers and green lawns. The Pickerings have done more to promote track in Britain than any other family. Shaun is now carrying on the job after both Ron and Jean passed

from left: Marni, Mary Toomey, Samantha and Joyce

away. Joyce, Marni and Corey, were fortunate to stay with Jean during the Montreal Olympics, while I was with the Saudi Arabian team.

Just recently I received a phone call from Bill. It was great to hear from him. We laughed and spoke of wonderful memories we share, he is good physical health, still active in the track world and is optimistic that he could help coach athletes in his area and is happy to live near his daughter Sarah in North Lake Tahoe.

FUN FACTS

He was born on the <u>tenth</u> of January…

Competed in the decathlon with <u>ten</u> events… for <u>ten</u> years

He set the decathlon record in the <u>tenth</u> month of the year… and his name has <u>ten</u> letters…

He must be Bill Toomey!

***Although I returned to Los Angeles after my one-year contract at UCSB had ended, Bill and I continued our coach-athlete relationship. In 1966, Joyce and I bought our first home in the then-sleepy town of Agoura. I had a scenic forty-five-minute commute along the Pacific Coast Highway to a wonderful teaching position at Palisades High School. After several years of hoping to start a family, our first daughter, Marni Ann, was born in October of 1967.

Vintage Toomey: Finishing the 1968 Olympic decathlon's final event, the 1,500 meters, late in the night of the 10-event competition's second day.

18. Bill Toomey winning the gold medal in the
Olympic decathlon in Mexico City, 1968.

PALISADES HIGH SCHOOL (1965-69)

It was widely recognized as one of the top schools in the LA district. Situated in one of the most affluent neighborhoods in Los Angeles, the school was known for its population of high-achieving students. Students at Pali Hi *really* wanted to learn, and they let you know right after the bell. Most of the kids came from homes where their parents encouraged discussion of current events and ideas at the dinner table. It was a joyful awakening for me to challenge such motivated and talented students. I attempted to match their interests and needs, with a goal of creating lessons that were both meaningful and relevant. I was fortunate to work with Rose Gilbert, our school's passionate English teacher. She invited me to observe her advanced English classes, where I was able to see an extraordinary educator who regularly inspired her students by demanding excellence. I realized then that teaching at Pali Hi required a special effort.

Almost forty years later, my supervisor at Pepperdine, Dr. Botsford, sent my student teachers to Palisades High, where I supervised them in their English and Social Studies assignments. I was curious to see if Rose Gilbert was still teaching in Room 204. When I went to the school to observe my student teachers, I looked into her classroom and saw the same piles of student essays dotting empty spaces and heard her familiar and unique voice. I also saw the same excitement in the students that I had witnessed so many years ago. Although Rose was at an age when most teachers had already retired, her teaching style was as intense and electric as ever. "I'm on fire," she told the *Los Angeles Times* in 2013. After fifty years of teaching, "She never seemed to burn out."

One of the teaching strategies that I enjoyed was to organize mock trials requiring each student to represent a personality who had a role in some historical event. For example, our class put Heinrich Himmler on trial in absentia for his role as a war criminal during World War II. The trial required two lawyers and a researcher for each side, six witnesses, one judge, one sergeant-at-arms, one recorder, two reporters, five students to make a program, and a video crew. One of my standout students, Cody Shearer, took on the challenging task by reading most of *The Rise and Fall of the Third Reich* for his background information as a witness for the prosecution. Sometimes I discovered that the most talented students seldom turned in homework but demonstrated extraordinary proficiency at defending their positions in oral arguments. When presented with the challenge of defending Himmler or receiving a low grade in my class, one such student organized a brilliant case in which his team shocked our class by earning an acquittal for Himmler. Our trial was held in the school's auditorium with an audience of parents and students from other US history classes. The next day, the *Los Angeles Times* ran an editorial criticizing the outcome. Another trial involved a Hispanic, Reyes Lopez Tijerina, for challenging the US government's right to take lands in New Mexico.

One of the most passionate trials took place during the Vietnam War. The topic was Agent Orange: a military necessity or a violation of international law. Students were energized as never before. The participants used nightly news reports, their own additional research, and guest speakers in order to present information that would support their positions. Our debates during lunchtime attracted students from other classes. The involvement of such a committed slice of our student population contributed to heated but productive discourse. It was inspiring to see so many students responding to our requests for thorough research and their willingness to apply the skills they learned outside of the classroom setting. It was the ultimate repudiation of the lecture-centered class. One noted educator, Noam Chomsky, said it best: "It doesn't matter what we cover this semester; it's what we *discover* as you are learning." During my stay at Pali Hi, our nation was involved in a highly unpopular war, especially for young men who were facing a possible draft. It was called a "police action," but had a profound effect on our country. Students demanded answers to the US involvement in Vietnam, often joining protest movements, burning draft cards, and sometimes denouncing their country. It was not unusual to see many of them gathered at Palisades Park for pro-and-con war rallies. Others wore black armbands in class, which were sometimes confiscated by teachers. Seniors exchanged strategies to avoid being drafted. It created a tense atmosphere in school, often pitting one teacher against another. Such a charged atmosphere made teaching more difficult, but my students learned a great deal about evaluating national and global events as history in the process of being made.

During that time, I continued coaching my runners after school, both at UCLA and at Pierce College. New runners joined us, including Olympians and college graduates from all over the United States. News travels quickly within the running community, and many were curious about experiencing the new Run for Fun philosophy that I had developed at Pierce College and UCSB. I put a lot of miles on my Volkswagen bug during that time. Looking back, I still find it difficult to explain how I was able to survive teaching in such a respected school environment as Palisades High in addition to coaching elite athletes.

The Southern California Striders was the oldest and best-organized track and field club in our area. Club leaders asked me to become their running coach and to help with organizational issues. These were among my most enjoyable and rewarding years as a track coach. I was thrilled when Jim Bush, the highly successful coach at UCLA, asked me to help his former NCAA champion miler, Bob Day, prepare for the 1968 Olympics. Bob had sustained a serious Achilles tendon injury and needed to be carefully guided if he ever hoped to return to competitive form. He would probably need to concentrate on the 5,000-meter race, since his injury would make it difficult to sustain the intense speed work needed for his former specialty, the 1,500-meter run. Bob was the most successful distance runner in UCLA history, and our group welcomed his infectious good humor and positive attitude. He was a prototypical Run for Fun athlete. In the words of Coach Jim Bush: "Pete took one of my greatest distance runners after he graduated. Bob had injured himself at the end of his senior year and needed an understanding coach to help him regain his strength and train for the 5,000-meter at Lake Tahoe. Getting Bob healthy and mentally ready for competition took a real coach." I had to adjust Bob's training schedule to avoid sprints while emphasizing short-rest, slower intervals. I regularly checked his heart rate to make sure he was physically handling my gradual introduction of faster and more intense intervals. All of my athletes ended their workouts by running 200 meters using a "swing stride" tempo, which was our terminology for a fast but relaxed and controlled effort. After weeks of struggling to run thirty seconds, it was exciting to see him glide through a twenty-six-second 200-meter sprint. At Lake Tahoe, he beat an outstanding field of athletes and earned a spot on the Olympic team.

Mark Winzenried from Wisconsin, a prolific and successful 800-meter runner, sometimes ran races in two separate meets on the same day. He would run a race in Germany in the morning and fly to Scandinavia for a twilight race. Our 1968 Olympic team was one of the best ever assembled. Eighteen Striders qualified for the team, including Bill Toomey, who won a gold medal, Ron Whitney, Bob Day, and John Bragg. We won the National AAU Outdoor Championships many times during those years. Our 4x100-meter relay team, which consisted of an American, a Guianese, a Panamanian, and Jamaican Don Quarrie, set a new world record.

19. Run for Fun training group in Santa Barbara. Top row from left; Ted Nelson, Pete and unknown 800 m runner. Bottom row from left; Ron Whitney and Mike Larrabee.

LAKE TAHOE AND THE MEXICO
OLYMPICS (1968)

Echo Summit, overlooking spectacular South Lake Tahoe, was perhaps the most unlikely site for any Olympic trials, but I believe that the decision to hold the 1968 trials at that site was a major factor in the success of our team. It was a truly unique setting and became a magical place for all of us. Top athletes who were determined to have a chance to make the team were invited to train and eventually compete for the coveted three places. South Lake was chosen because of its 6800-foot altitude—close but not equal to the 7200-foot altitude of Mexico City.

The track and training facility was the brainchild of Walt Little, the parks director of South Lake and a sports writer. Walt became the driving force for the project, easily winning support from everyone around the lake. With Payton Jordan, the Olympic coach, supporting the idea, and a five-cent motel tax and Harrah's Hotel providing financial backing, enough money was raised to build the track and the athlete's trailers. The park service granted the Olympic committee permission to cut down some trees in El Dorado Park, so that a track could be built around and through the trees. The new synthetic track was carved out of the rocks, with remaining trees and a few leftover boulders spread throughout the infield. It was ironic that the relaxing and serene setting at Echo Summit would provide the backdrop for some of the most intense competition in Olympic history.

Carlos Harlan described the facility in the *Tahoe Quarterly*: "Imagine a state-of-the-art synthetic track nestled in the rugged woods above Lake Tahoe, overlooked by fans perched on granite boulders, watching anxiously for the world's best sprinters to burst through the woods."

20. Echo Summit at Lake Tahoe, California - site of the Olympic Track and field trials, 1968.

I was fortunate to have been chosen by Bill Bowerman as one of the distance-running coaches. Joyce and I were provided an apartment for the lead-up to the trials and the Olympics, which made for an exciting summer for our family. I was humbled that he had selected me for the position, especially since it meant that the successes of my current and former athletes had been recognized. It was a thrilling experience to be able to oversee the training of our best distance runners, including Marty Liquori, Bob Day, Mike Manley, Mark Winzenried and others. I could also continue working with Bill Toomey and Ron Whitney, while being able to watch our Strider pole-vaulters, John Pennel and Bob Seagren, clear record heights. With such legends as John Carlos, Tommie Smith, and Ralph Boston all competing against the best challengers in the country, it provided a setting for one of our most competitive trials. Only the most dedicated athletes and those who truly embraced the rigors of training and competing were able to survive.

A WELCOME TO LOS ANGELES,
by Mike Manley, Eugene, Oregon

I first met "Pete" shortly after I returned from Vietnam in April of 1968. He was coaching a group of runners, many of whom belonged to the Southern California Striders. Pat Traynor, one of the top steeplechasers in the country, was in Pete's group and invited me to join them. I was delighted to have someone to train with, especially since my wife, Connie, and I had just driven from Wisconsin and knew very few people in Los Angeles at the time.

As most distance runners know, having other runners with whom to train is useful in lessening the grind of training that is required to excel at that level. But having a coach who can provide the guidance, offer useful suggestions, and give the encouragement needed to be successful is key. Pete had all of that and much more. He could communicate with all kinds of personalities no matter which type filled the shorts and shoes of those young men and women standing or running in front of him.

Pete was able to effectively manage the competition that invariably occurs among fiercely competitive runners during training sessions. One technique, I remember, was using a grass field venue on the UCLA campus for frequent training sessions. During those sessions, no watch was used to time our efforts. He gave us specific patterns to run on the field and specific instructions on how each was to be run. I called the workout: I's, L's, U's, J's, O's, and dashes, because it was a workout consisting of different speeds and tempos. I used the same technique during my thirty-five-plus years of coaching runners.

While I had the good fortune of being coached by Pete, I didn't make it to the Olympic Games in 1968. It was a big disappointment because Pete had done so much for me during our five months of working together. He did his job well. I was ready. I just didn't perform as I should have. After the US Olympic trials in Tahoe, I moved to Eugene, Oregon, where I had previously registered for the teacher-training curriculum at the University of Oregon.

Pete was a teacher of boys, girls, men, and women, and he still is to this day. Pete didn't coach for a living; he was a social studies teacher. But he loved the sport and loved helping his athletes, as well as his students, prepare for their future successes.

I learned many valuable lessons from Pete. I don't know how many times I heard, "Relax, train, don't strain," and, "The only difference between run and fun is the first letter," and, "You can do it, Mike. Go get 'em." For four years those words reverberated in my ears as I trained, raced, and finally made it to the Olympics in 1972.

Thanks, Pete. And thanks, also, for the suggestions and lesson plans you sent me for some of the social studies classes I taught in Eugene for thirty years.

21. Mike Manley winning a mile race at Echo Summit while preparing for 1968 Olympics.

Steve Simmons, the next Olympic coach, described it best: "You had the cream of the crop out there. It was cutthroat, like a war. If you didn't make it, they sent your butt home the next day. They gave you a ticket, drove you down to Reno, and you were out of there." A fourth-place finish was like a death sentence.

Ask Bill Toomey after his fourth-place finish in the 1964 trials, or ask Mark Winzenried, who, by the narrowest of margins, placed fourth in the 800-meter.

The fierce competition produced results. In Mexico City, our athletes set three world records and hauled in twenty-four medals. Bob Beamon, Bob Seagren, Al Oerter, Dick Fosbury, John Pennel, Jimmy Hines, Willie Davenport, Geoff Vanderstock, Ron Whitney, George Young, and Lee Evans made track-and-field history.

THOSE WERE THE DAYS,
by Ron Whitney, Glen Ellen, California

I have known Pete for a long time…Everyone knows Pete, don't they? If you don't, you really need to. My first recollection is still clear. As a recent Oxy graduate (recent, as in 1964!), I had just completed my warm-up for the LA indoor 600-meter when this stranger approached me wearing a Cheshire cat smile and wished me luck. He reminded me to "have fun." Have fun? Are you crazy? There is no fun in racing, just fear and terror…Who is this guy, anyway? That was the beginning.

I soon realized that Pete wore the same smile each time we met. He was that way with everyone…all the time…He must even sleep with the same look…His eternal optimism accompanied his smile and soon became infectious, winning over everyone he encountered. For Chrissake, he even wrote a book, Run for Fun, and spent much of his Southern California Strider volunteer "no pay" purchasing and giving out T-shirts advertising his philosophy.

Those were the days, my friend. We were surrounded by a team of Olympians, world-record holders, and past, present, and future elites of our sport, who together could beat most other countries. Pete was right in the middle of it all, encouraging us to "enjoy the race," followed by congratulations or reassurance, depending on the outcome. Yep, this was the big time: $2.00 a day per diem if you made a US team, and free plane tickets (complimentary peanuts included), hotel, and food. What could be better? One might say Pete was the leader of "socialized sport." Everyone got the same $2.00, worked full time, and trained when they could, very few prospering from their athletic endeavors. Pete was the "Latvian Socialist"…and we loved it all!

I have been fortunate to know Pete and his wife Joyce off the track, as well. We shared an apartment at Bavarian Village for a short time before the final 1968 trials at Tahoe, played in the snow along with other team members, mates, and friends at my folks' place, and continue to keep in touch. In some ways, absolutely nothing has *changed with Pete; he still wears the smile, shares his same encouragement with student teachers, maintains contacts with masses of friends, and has just chronicled his incredible life's adventures in written form. How lucky I have been to witness and share in his sunshine.*

It didn't take long for all of us to feel the effects of the high altitude. Runners had to make adjustments, since the altitude affected everyone differently. You had to treat some athletes with kid gloves. We had to reexamine our training routines, especially when trying to add high-intensity interval workouts to the training schedule. All-out sprints sometimes caused an athlete's system to react completely different from what was normally experienced at sea level. Jim Ryun had an especially difficult experience. The altitude, dry air, and unfiltered sun exacerbated the need to take in sufficient liquids. Marty Liquori had difficulty falling asleep, so I advised him to drink a beer in the evening, which motivated his mother to let me know what she thought of the idea. However unorthodox, apparently the beer therapy worked, since Marty later ran a mile in less than four minutes in Eugene and made the Olympic team.

The Tahoe area is famous for challenging running trails and scenic views. Most of our training runs were between altitudes of six thousand to eight thousand feet. Gerry Lindgren led our group on one memorable run, where a smooth trail abruptly changed into a rocky, unmarked wilderness, and we found ourselves surrounded by thorny scrub. Gerry, the same fanatical runner who endured 240-mile weeks, would be the last to succumb to the conditions. With our legs festooned with scrapes and bruises, most of us abandoned the run, leaving Gerry on his own. He returned to camp an hour later with a smile on his face. He was the perfect example of a Run for Fun athlete. Unfortunately, he paid a price for his lack of caution, having injured an Achilles tendon, which slowed him considerably in the 10,000-meter trials.

Although I had the pleasure of working with many outstanding distance runners at Tahoe, Marty Liquori was unique. He was a nineteen-year-old freshman out of Villanova who had yet to compete in an intercollegiate race (college freshmen did not compete in varsity events). I was impressed with his confidence and his eagerness to face older and more experienced runners. Facing elite middle-distance runners in an open meet in Bakersfield, he proved that he could run with the best, recording the second sub-four-minute mile while still in high school. Years later, I watched him win both the NCAA and AAU championships while at Villanova. He went on to face the best runners in the world in Europe, leaving no doubts about his competitiveness and earning him the number-one ranking in the world in mile and 1,500-meter races in 1969 and 1971. Six years later he established a reputation for versatility with a number-one ranking in the 5,000-meter race. Back home, his most noteworthy win came in the much-anticipated duel in the "Dream Mile" in Philadelphia, beating Jim Ryun by a step. He was an obvious selection to the National Distance Running Hall of Fame.

I'm sure having Jumbo Elliott as his coach helped him develop his impressive consistency. He was inspired by Elliot's approach to life, training, and personal qualities. Marty described him best: "His method is a mixed bag—an eclectic blend of showmanship, salesmanship, Irish wit and blarney, parental care, discipline, and knowledge. He inspired confidence."

You can imagine how happy I was when Elliott, in his absence, asked me to take over as Marty's coach at the trials. This gave Joyce and me an opportunity to get to know Marty and his wife. With every passing day, and after many training sessions, we developed a mutual respect. Our relationship enabled me to explore ways to design the best workouts for him while continuing his established training routines (don't tamper with success). Both of us agreed that a runner performs best by training hard, but also conceded that resting before races was necessary to be physically and mentally fresh for competition. At that late time, there was no need to intensify his workouts with hopes of gaining more conditioning, but to instead maintain quality of effort. I was happy when he told me that he relied on heart rate, which never exceeded 170 beats per minute, as a means of determining his conditioning. Although I didn't have the high-tech monitors that coaches use today, I used a watch-timed heart rate measurement extensively with my runners during our training sessions. I was inspired by Kenny Moore's excellent segment on the Finnish runners in *Sports Illustrated.*

Both of us were aware that the altitude would affect our training, but Marty seldom expressed concerns. He had the advantage of being comfortable with the utilization of longer, sustained efforts, rather than sudden, quick injections of sprints, which caused many runners to lose their form as they gasped for air. He seldom lost a race in the homestretch. From then on, I used him as a role model for my runners.

His mature and confident attitude enabled him to deal with the altitude at Mexico City: just go out and run your race, no matter how many Kenyans are there. He survived the heats and felt confident that he could earn a medal. But luck was not on his side when he started to feel the pain of a stress fracture before the final, thus ending his Olympic quest on a sad note. He could take solace in the fact that he was the youngest 1,500-meter finalist in Olympic history.

We were able to keep in touch after the Mexico Olympics. Whenever he visited Southern California, Hank Ehrlich of the Southern California Striders treated us to dinners, arranged a guest appearance on TV, and took us to Paramount movie previews. I was delighted when NBC chose Marty as one of the announcers for the 1972, 1976, and 1984 Olympic marathons and other sports events. His low-key tone, personable demeanor, and extensive knowledge of the backgrounds of athletes proved to be a welcome addition to the network coverage of the games. After his retirement from athletic completion, he went on to successful careers in retail sales (Athletic Attack stores), as a commentator-announcer, and finally as a talented musician.

TRAINING FOR THE 1968 MEXICO CITY OLYMPICS, by Marty Liquori, Gainesville, Florida

I am not sure when I first met Pete. I do know in retrospect that it was not a moment too soon. Had it been a few weeks later, I know I would not have made the 1968 US Olympic Team. It was an honor to compete in Mexico City, my one and only Olympics as a competitor.

Pete took over my coaching about two months before the final Olympic trials. I did not find out until many years later why my college coach, Jumbo Elliott, turned me over to Pete Petersons so completely just before the Olympic trials. The official story was that Jumbo and Pete were coaching me 'jointly'. Jumbo just said that Pete was on-site and I should work with him. What I found out about 30 years later was that Jumbo had suffered a stroke and kept it a secret so as to not hurt recruiting. He was unable to devote the time and travel to my quest and Jumbo was ego-less enough to turn me over to Pete.

So I started working with Pete, who was able to evaluate my strengths and weaknesses, and give me the finishing speed that I lacked, which enabled me to make the Olympic team. Pete's philosophy was much different than the one I had been brought up with in high school and college, where running was full-out every workout. You were hurting almost the whole time and dreading the next track workout. Pete's philosophy of "Run for Fun" changed my outlook on training for the rest of my life, enabling me to have a much longer and enjoyable career. His emphasis on running in shorter bursts of speed changed me as a runner. There's only so much you can do with a person's natural talent and I never became a really fast finisher, but I got fast enough to hold the last 15 yards that I would have coming off the final turn.

This all happened in 1968, the end of my freshman year in college. The next year, I was rated number one in the world, and again in 1971. In 1972 I graduated from college and made the toughest decision of my life, which I continue to this day to question more than any other. I had to decide whether to move Santa Barbara for training with Pete or move to Gainesville, Florida to attend graduate school in Journalism at the University of Florida. If the University of California in Santa Barbara had a graduate program for Journalism, I probably would have gone there. The main reason I stayed on the East coast was because my family was there and I felt that if there was an emergency, I could drive from Florida back to New Jersey overnight. To me, at 22, my parents were really old ......they were about 50.

So I moved to Gainesville and had a great life! Had I not moved to Gainesville, I doubt I would have ever started an athletic shoe store (Athletic Attic) which was "Berry Berry good to me", as the saying goes. However, even 40 years later, there are very few humid days during the summer when I don't say "Damn it, I should have moved to Santa Barbara!"

Pete and I went on to be good friends and have many wonderful conversations and good times. Pete's always-positive attitude and joie-de-vive was catching and much needed by an over-thinking athlete who thought he was under a lot of pressure to succeed. We had many amazing experiences at the European track meets. This is something that I came to realize no amount of money could duplicate. This friendship and time spent with a very special person was the gift that was the main reward for our hard work to get on the "European Track and Field Circuit". Athletes today make a lot *of money doing what we did, but I wouldn't trade what they have for what we had when we "Ran For Fun."*

The South Lake training facility marked the beginning of a new era of research into the effects of high altitude on athletic performance. Coaches and medical staff saw a unique study population that could be used to thoroughly explore the benefits and challenges of training in an environment of reduced oxygen pressure. It would turn out to be a pioneering experiment in exercise physiology. Mexico City provided the motivation to investigate the premise that high altitude training for American athletes, especially distance runners, could provide a means of equalizing the advantage enjoyed by the Kenyans, whose ability to perform at high altitude had been developed on a genetic level for millions of years. The 1,500-meter battle between Kip Keino and Jim Ryun was the best example of what was at stake. Although one example was not definitive, Ryun's loss to the Kenyan was evidence that six weeks of training at high altitude could not cancel out the built-in advantages of the Africans. Sprinters and jumpers, however, loved the thinner air, as evidenced by Bob Beamon's spectacular world-record-breaking long jump.

The civil rights movement became part of the Olympic narrative. Racial tensions were at modern highs, but the athletes tried to remain focused on their training. The fact that athletes were able to share housing with their wives did a lot to maintain good morale. Married athletes stayed in motels by the lake, while singles were housed in trailers across Highway 50. A kitchen prepared quality food for all of the athletes. Ed Burke, a three-time Olympian in the hammer throw, described the Tahoe experience: "You'd get up, probably eat a steak and eggs, go lift weights, lay on the pole vault pit in the warm sun and watch airplanes, and then do nothing." For recreation, they could try to negotiate the treacherous, winding drive "down the hill" to visit stores, play golf, and test their luck in Harrah's Casino. Tom Von Ruden and John Carlos ended up working at the casino. I enjoyed spending time with Bill Toomey, John Pennel, and Ron Whitney.

They had a weird way of dealing with the tension of competition. They wandered through the forest, talking to the trees as if they were people, telling jokes, imitating Jonathan Winters, Red Skelton, or Donald Duck. I wish I could have recorded their conversations so, forty years later, we could all be entertained by their antics.

Most of the athletes at the training facility treasured their experience in the beautiful California mountains. Even Tommie Smith, who grew up in Texas where there were few fir trees, became emotional when our Tahoe experience came to an end. Unfortunately, I was unable to travel to Mexico City to see my athletes compete. I had to return to my job at Palisades for the new school semester.

For Joyce, Marni (2), and myself, our adventure in Lake Tahoe continued the following year when Walt Little invited me to organize an all-comers meet at the intermediary school, where the Olympic training track was relocated. Many of the Olympians returned to relive the Tahoe experience. I helped Lee Evans, the Olympic 400-meter gold medal winner, with a training program designed to enable him to break his own record. I supervised his training and helped with the timing of his track sessions. Unfortunately, adrenaline got the best of him, and he ran his first 200 meters too fast to finish in record time.

Another development that caught the IAAF by surprise in 1969 was when Puma produced a revolutionary new track shoe with sixty-eight separate needle spikes, instead of the usual eight large spikes. It gave sprinters added gripping power on the track surface. Lee Evans set a new world record, but the IAAF refused to recognize it. After the smoke had cleared, track's governing body outlawed the needle-spike shoes.

THE OLYMPICS AND THE
END OF AMATEURISM

We have seen a renaissance in American distance running. Unlike the past, many have continued running well past their college years. Marathon runners and their coaches have relocated to high-altitude locations such as Mammoth, California; Boulder, Colorado; and Flagstaff, Arizona. They are able to reap the benefits of year-round training at high altitude. They sometimes ran 120-mile weeks interspersed with shorter-distance speed-training sessions at lower altitudes. Because of generous financial support from shoe companies, runners are now able to concentrate entirely on running, instead of juggling part-time jobs in an effort to pay the rent and keep food on the table. Most elite runners are guided by excellent coaches such as Alberto Salazar, Mark Wetmore, Bob Larsen, Joe Wehill, and John Shumacher. The results have been impressive, with many winning medals in the Olympics and World Championships. Both Dena Drosin and Meb Keflezighi won Olympic marathon bronze medals and recently destroyed an international field of runners in Boston, something unheard of twenty years ago.

The Rome Olympics in 1960 marked the beginning of a new era in public perception of track and field. ABC televised the games for the first time, and its *Wide World of Sports* gave the American public an opportunity to see athletes as individuals with unique personalities. Frank Shorter's marathon victory at Munich in 1972 gave birth to a running boom that swept the country during the decade that followed. After Mexico and Munich, the presence of US athletes helped attract big crowds in Europe. The insatiable European demand for elite athletes strained the established boundaries of amateurism.

The Mexico Olympics marked the beginning of the end for amateurism. It had been forbidden to accept money, meals, or even an appearance on a TV show. One of my Strider long jumpers was stripped of his amateur status because he received a salary as a physical education teacher. Bill Toomey appeared on a game show, but the money he received had to be "donated" to the amateur association. Lee Calhoun, the odds-on favorite to win the 110-meter hurdles in Rome, was disqualified because he appeared on a newlywed show. Such outmoded policies were deemed impractical and extreme. As track meets were becoming more popular and bringing in more television revenue, athletes began to question why they were not able to share in the revenue created by 50,000–75,000 spectators crammed into venues like the Berlin Olympic stadium. They began to defy the rules by demanding "appearance fees." After all, they were responsible for the large crowds that filled the stadium, and reasonably assumed that they should receive a share of the revenue. To appease the big names, meet directors arranged for payments to be made to the athlete's agents, often under the grandstands. Olympian Mal Whitfield was once unhappy with the promised fee for his 800-meter race, so he stopped at 600 meters while leading the race, saying, "You paid me less, so I ran less of the distance." He received his normal fee the next race with no arguments. It was not a surprise the see a redefinition of amateurism after the Mexico Olympics.

To me, the idea of "running for money" was still alien. None of my athletes demanded payments. They simply enjoyed the spirit of competition. My Run for Fun T-shirts symbolized my involvement in the sport. My runners wore them as a statement that proclaimed our motivation for participating. One of our Strider shot putters, a world-record holder and Olympic medalist, kiddingly asked me to print a "Chuck for Buck" shirt.

The shoe companies (Nike, Adidas, Puma) had not yet started recruiting top athletes, although they provided shoes and apparel for their stars. Eventually, they wanted to sponsor almost any athlete who had competed in national championships. I witnessed athletes carrying armloads of gear from Puma headquarters directly to Adidas and walking away with equipment bearing a three-stripe logo. Adidas stopped this practice when John Bragg and Mike Larrabee posted names of athletes who were *not* invited to meets, since they were already associating with Puma. Some even attempted to be loyal to both by wearing a Puma shoe on one foot and Adidas on the other. Others who were not under contract to Nike, but liked their Nike spikes for races, sometimes tore the logo off of their shoes. If they performed well, they hoped to nail down a contract.

The Munich Olympics offered a promotional opportunity that could not be overlooked by Puma and Nike. We watched in disbelief as Mark Spitz waved Puma shoes on the victory stand, as if they played a part in helping him win his seven swimming medals. The shoe and athletic apparel companies continued to exploit and expand the advertising audiences generated by the Olympics. The 1984 Olympics made Carl Lewis an instant star. My good friend Joe Douglas, from Santa Monica Track Club, orchestrated Carl's exposure to the media, even demanding payments if the press wanted to take his picture. Eventually Joe was able to set a price of up to $100,000 for the top European meets. Today that is a normal fee for Usain Bolt.

With Olympics becoming a lucrative revenue-generating venue for athletes and coaches, many found it hard to resist the temptation to use performance-enhancing drugs (steroids), blood doping, or "masking" agents to cover up the abuses. A coach from Los Angeles came up with the idea of eating garlic and onion slices before his athletes were to be tested, hoping it would somehow mask the drugs. Racing on the track morphed into a race between drug violators and medical personnel. Could medical experts keep up with the developers of difficult-to-detect drugs? The athletes who attempted to seek "better performance through chemistry" tended to disappear for months in Mexico and became prime targets for testing. Some weight-event athletes used "andro" (androstenedione) drugs for gaining weight and strength. Lance Armstrong and Tour de France violators loved the "EPO" (erythropoietin) cocktail, which resulted in more red cell production. The Finns found success in "blood doping" (removing some blood and then reinjecting it before major competitions). By increasing the density of red blood cells, athletes could use the added oxygen to fight off the accumulation of lactic acid. Some women sprinters experimented with growth hormones, while others took a year off in order to have a baby, hoping to gain strength and maturity. These high-risk activities continue today, but blood testing mandated by the IOC and athletic federations of various countries has progressed to sophisticated levels. It is not unusual to have some athletes tested repeatedly if their performances are consistently exceptional or have shown unusual improvement over past marks. Usain Bolt, for example, was tested over fifty times this year alone, and found to be clean. Testing is performed unannounced to athletes, so they can be awakened from sleep, attending school, or vacationing. Athletes now have to announce ahead of time where they can be found. They can no longer travel to remote locations to train while taking PEDs (Performance Enhancing Drugs). Such sneaky, but effective, cat-and-mouse games take place even as you read this story.

Most of us probably remember the first big violator, Ben Johnson, who was (finally) found guilty of using steroids in the 1980 Seoul Olympics. Investigations have revealed that the East Germans were flagrant drug abusers during the 1960s and 1970s. Their female sprinters set records that still stand. If they wanted to compete, their athletes had no choice but to cooperate with their coaches and their national federation. Since those dark days of not-so-secret drug use, hundreds of top athletes have been exposed. For me, the saddest part is that I have known many of them as good friends. Marion Jones didn't need drugs; she was a naturally gifted athlete who could have excelled without them. I watched her compete in high-school meets, long jumping well over twenty-one feet and destroying her opponents in sprints. I was saddened when Tyson Gay, a record holder and Olympic silver medalist in the 100-meter, admitted his guilt in 2015. All this took place after he had started a movement among athletes to "compete clean." Such is the result of athletes seeking fame and wealth. The "end justifies the means" lives on.

CLUB WEST AND COACHING
TRAVELS (1969-75)

VENEZUELA TOUR (1969)

"**B**ud" Winters, the coach at San Jose State, is famous for his success with sprinters, with John Carlos and Tommy Smith being two of his most famous protégées. Joyce and I will always hold him in high regard as a coach and as a wonderful human being. He invited me to assist him in a track clinic in Venezuela and made sure Joyce and our young daughter Marni could join us. Watching him coach young Venezuelan athletes was like watching comedian Robin Williams explaining the proper form of sprinting techniques. In his first encounter, he lined up the runners and asked them to run as fast as possible, emphasizing the use of exaggerated arm and leg movement. He asked me to illustrate, so I poured out all my energy, arms flailing while my body leaned backward, my face showing obvious strain. Coach Winters told each runner his time after that initial all-out effort. He then followed with a demonstration of proper technique and sprinting without straining every muscle. The runners lined up for another trial, this time with instructions to run hard, but *not* all-out. Every one of them ran faster. From then on, our clinic was a huge success. Sprinters followed him as if he was the Pied Piper. He engaged shot putters the same way. Bud gave the athletes instructions for proper form, and we tried to control our amusement while watching an athlete awkwardly search under his chin or next to his ear for a suitable place to begin the throwing motion. As a concluding test of our athletes training efforts, we attended the *Bolivariano Games* in Maracaibo (in honor of Simon Bolivar). Arthur Lydiard, the legendary coach from New Zealand, joined our group and introduced distance runners to his "marathon" training methods. All of the long-distance runners today base their success, at least partially, on adding mileage in order to gain more cardiovascular conditioning. It is a common practice today for athletes to run up to 120 miles per week, with some pushing it to an incredible 150 miles. Coach Lydiard asked me to go for a run in the ninety-plus-degrees heat and stifling humidity that is typical near Lake Maracaibo's oil-drilling region. I survived a five-mile run, but just barely. Every time I wanted to stop or slow down, he insisted that I keep running, no matter how slow. He compared the running motion to pumping air into a tire, not letting any air escape when stopping to rest. One of our athletes asked him what was the best way to breathe while running. His reply was simple, "If you can suck in air through your mouth, toes, or even your ears, do it." His no-nonsense approach to running was creative but logical. He was always a gentleman, and I learned a great deal from Arthur. We enjoyed dinners with Bud and his wife Helen. Bud became especially excited whenever the conversation involved food and restaurants. He loved fine dining and took every opportunity to evaluate local eateries. He always had recommendations for the best dishes on a menu: the best clam chowder, best steak, best cordon bleu, best veal piccata, etc. Apparently, he was gathering material for a book on "My Favorite Dishes." Calamari was the one dish that he felt few local restaurants were able to prepare adequately. He remained optimistic and was hopeful that we could find such a restaurant in Caracas, but despite his efforts, we had no luck. He shrugged it off in his own nonchalant way, muttering to himself that he should perhaps open a seafood restaurant in Caracas so people could taste such a superb dish. We loved him and will always remember Bud for his infectious humor and enthusiasm.

22. Marni, Pete and Joyce in Caracas, Venezuela, 1970.

MOVE TO SANTA BARBARA, 1970

I had spent five years coaching the Southern California Striders. Each day after school, I drove to UCLA or the Valley to work with my athletes. The teaching experience at Palisades, however, was about to undergo a big change. The Los Angeles city schools started a controversial bussing program in 1970. The school atmosphere had gone from exciting to uncomfortably tense in the course of a year. When my continuing association with Bill Toomey promised to develop into a new coaching opportunity in Santa Barbara, Joyce and I decided to move once again. We bought a new home in Santa Barbara, and I got a job at La Colina Junior High School.

Bill Toomey's success at Mexico City and the near-perfect training climate of Santa Barbara motivated us to consider the possibility of forming our own club. Having a core group of outstanding athletes in the same training venue was exciting to me. When Jim and Anne Ryun added their support, the pieces began to fall into place. With backing from the city of Goleta, Club West was born. We were a Santa Barbara club, not to be confused with Nike's Portland-based Athletics West. Once the word got out that Santa Barbara was the new mecca for elite track athletes, we were joined by an impressive group of new arrivals. I had already started coaching NCAA 800-meter champ, Mark Winzenried. Mark was soon joined by Terry Harrison (distances), Jere Van Dyk (Oregon's great miler), and Jerome Liebenberg. Bill's success in the multi-events attracted new training partners in Russ Hodge, Dave Thoreson, John Warkentin, and Harry Marra, which made Santa Barbara the US center of multi-event development. Sam Adams, the UCSB coach, was responsible for allowing our athletes access to the university facilities and graciously helped to provide technical and logistical support. His background in the weight events proved to be invaluable. Unfortunately, our club existed before the era of mega-sponsorship by shoe companies, and our athletes found it difficult to earn enough money to support themselves in expensive Santa Barbara. After two years, our dream club ceased to exist, so we sold our home and moved back to Agoura. Both Joyce and I were fortunate to get fabulous teaching positions in the Las Virgenes school district, so we purchased the home that we continue to live in today. Our second daughter, Corey was born in 1974, and I was able to resume coaching the Southern California Striders at UCLA and Pierce.

PETE AND CLUB WEST,
by Harry Marra, Eugene, Oregon

I was a decathlete with Club West in Santa Barbara, California from 1971 to 1973. I was an average athlete at best, but both Bill Toomey and Coach Pete Petersons welcomed me with open arms. It was a marvelous two-year experience for me, where a large part of the philosophies and foundations that I use today as a coach were firmly implanted into my psyche.

Sam Adams was my primary coach at that time, but I had numerous interactions with Pete, especially observing him each day while he was working with world-class athletes like Jim Ryun, Mark Winzenried, Jere Van Dyk, and so many others who were all part of Club West during those years. His mannerisms and his devotion to his profession impressed upon me at that young age just how coaching was meant to be carried out. It was in Santa Barbara, in the spring of 1972, when a light went on for me that this thing called coaching was what I wanted to do with my life. Coach Pete Petersons played an important part in my making that life decision.

Pete was the complete coach—very knowledgeable in his craft, completely supportive of his athletes, organized, and an ever-present smile on his face. With his upbeat attitude, he made tough workouts light, fun, and enjoyable. It impressed me.

On a funny note, I will always remember Pete by one word: BEEEEEP! Coach Petersons did not use a whistle to mark the time of a specific split for his runners; he did not use a megaphone…he simply let loose with a high, shrill BEEEEEP at the exact split time. You could hear this all over the track and into the Isla Vista community that borders the UCSB track facility. I still have great memories from that great time in my life, being surrounded by great people like Coach Pete Petersons.

COACHING TRAVELS OVERSEAS:
1973 US TEAM TOUR

I along with nearly everyone who has ever worked with track athletes, had always dreamed of being named as a coach of a US touring team. The 1973 tour to Russia and Africa was especially rewarding, since it followed so closely after the Munich Olympics and included many of our Olympians. I was delighted to see Jim Bush named as a coach (In my opinion, he should have been named the head Olympic coach!). I was pleased to be voted in as an assistant to Jim. He had unselfishly helped with many of our Southern California Strider athletes. Our touring group also consisted of Dr. Daly and Dr. Jerome Bornstein, who acted as medical consultants. Many of our Olympians welcomed the opportunity to return to Europe. Dwight Stones, an elite high jumper, was especially eager to have another opportunity to set the new world record that had eluded him in 1972. Despite rainy conditions, Dwight achieved his goal. My role was to help Jim and our distance runners as a consultant and a "troubleshooter."

After Munich we flew to Minsk, the capital of Belarus, which for many of us would be our first meet in an Eastern European country. We arrived groggy from jet lag, but we knew that travel in a Communist country would present many uncertainties: strange foods, spartan accommodations, unreliable availability of training facilities, and the ever-suspicious local government officials. Fearing that our rooms might be bugged, we warned our athletes to be especially careful about what they said both privately and in public. Our food was adequate, but a far cry from home cooking. As a surprise, our teen sensation, Mary Decker, who excelled at long distances, requested and was able to get her favorite pre-meet meal of pasta. Athletes were frequently awakened by loud, squealing noises from the pipes every time someone in the hotel used the bathroom. We were taken on a tour to a huge tractor factory, but were warned not to take pictures of any part of the factory or even the rows of the shiny new red machines. Our young guide, who spoke perfect English, never missed an opportunity to praise their system, usually with false dates and obvious exaggeration. We were taken to a sacred monument that commemorated a tragedy during which the Germans locked 110 children into a church before setting fire to it. Dozens of bells of varying sizes could be seen scattered throughout the large area. Their ringing produced a variety of eerie sounds, making us reflect upon the suffering of the young victims. I found out that Janis Lusis, the legendary Olympic champion javelin thrower from Latvia, was among the athletes who would be competing in the meet. He had to represent Russia, since Latvia was no longer a nation. I set up a meeting with him and brought a bottle of bourbon, which I thought would cheer him up, but he was nevertheless reluctant to discuss life in Latvia.

Our last stop in Senegal presented a dilemma, especially for our African American athletes. None of us had ever been to Africa before and barely knew where Senegal was located. I knew from my experience as a history teacher that it was once a French colony, where people spoke and read French, drove Citroens, and flew in

Air France planes. The Senegalese seemed like citizens of France, which was a far cry from what our athletes expected.

As we approached the impressive Air France hotel, we felt relieved that our lodging would be more than satisfactory. Our relief was short-lived, as we were directed away from the hotel to the simple huts that were to be our designated housing. Each coach was assigned to his own hut, which gave us a moment of privacy after a long, arduous trip. The floor of each hut was festooned with thick rugs, and the bed was enveloped in mosquito netting, which was much appreciated. There was a large, nasty population of these creatures with which I didn't want to share my sleeping quarters. Senegal was the first African nation to install an all-weather tartan track that was good enough for international competitions. The distance runners knew that their work was cut out for them. With Commonwealth champion Filbert Bayi from Tanzania in the field, the 1,500 meters was the featured race of the meet. Bayi was notorious as a front-runner who enjoyed pushing the pace, usually leaving the field behind after two laps, although he sometimes barely held on at the finish. Sadly, he suffered from frequent malaria bouts, which prevented him from competing in the Olympics.

The highlight of our African tour was a visit to the infamous *island* of *Gorée, which* lies off the coast of Senegal, as short boat ride from Dakar. From the 15th to the 19th century, it was the largest slave-trading center on the African coast, the last stop for the thousands of slaves who were sold to white slave traders, who shipped them in slave ships heading to the Americas. Slaves were held for three months, living in barbaric holding rooms before they entered the "Door of no return". During the slave market, the slaves were paraded naked in front of the traders while the negotiating went on. It was a moving experience to be in that place, where time seemed to stand still, especially for our black athletes.

Many of the world leaders, including most American presidents have made a point of visiting this historic site.

PETE AND THE STRIDERS,
by Jim Bush, Los Angeles, California

I'm honored to write about Pete, whom I have known for almost forty years. I've known him to be an extraordinary teacher, and I consider him to be of the finest coaches in the country. He is willing to help any athlete who seeks his guidance, and he is especially good with distance runners. When I coached track at UCLA, we invited Pete's LA Striders group to train on our track after our team had finished. I saw firsthand the skill Pete displayed with his athletes, and I always encouraged my Bruins to join the Striders after they left UCLA.

Pete took Bob Day, one of my greatest distance runners, and helped him regain the form he had lost after a bad injury. He did such a great job that Bob won the 5,000-meter race at the 1968 Olympic trials. Pete's patience and encouragement was instrumental in Bob's recovery.

As head coach of the 1973 US track team that spent thirty days touring four countries (Germany, Italy, Russia, and Africa), I was privileged to have Pete as one of our team managers. When one of my distance runners specifically requested Pete to coach him, I readily agreed, knowing that my runner would be under the best of care. He gave Pete the medal that he won in one of his races, a normally rare gesture that typifies the appreciation the athletes had for the man.

Pete is one of the rare "old school" track personalities: he shares my view that the ultimate reward from coaching track and field is not monetary, but the excitement we feel when we see young men achieve success. He and his beautiful wife, Joyce, are two of the nicest people I have ever known. We were both blessed to be involved in a sport that brought so much fulfillment to our lives.

SAUDI ARABIA (1976)

One day in 1975, I received a call from Bill Toomey, who asked if I wanted to go to Saudi Arabia to coach distance runners. For a minute, I thought he was playing a trick on me with such an outrageous proposal. Whittaker Corporation had been awarded a contract to hire coaches from various sports to help develop Saudi athletic programs and, hopefully, prepare their athletes for the Montreal Olympics.

The thought of relocating my family to such a distant and strange environment put a scare into Joyce and me. We knew that Saudi Arabia practiced one of the world's most extreme versions of Islam and was especially restrictive for women. From the information I was able find, we would have to tolerate a country in which there is no separation of church and state. Saudi society is governed by Islamic law, which its citizens accept as the defining force in shaping their past and future, a situation that would be completely alien to an American. Tourists were not allowed to visit Saudi Arabia. The only foreigners allowed to live in the country were affiliated with established businesses, especially petroleum, telecommunications, and medical. To Joyce and me, it seemed ridiculous to give up my teaching job and uproot our family from a satisfying and comfortable life in Agoura. Joyce and I both knew that I was fortunate to teach in such a great school so close to home. We agonized as to how we would approach the district officials in order to request an extended leave. We could view the opportunity as an adventure and a chance to travel to new places, but we would still need to take care of the underlying issues of leaving a good job and a comfortable home. Joyce had a million questions: how would we deal with the strict Moslem rules, locate an adequate school for Marni, and negotiate the inevitable difficulties with language and customs? How would we adjust to foreign foods, and most important, find a decent place to live?

We were assured that we would be working with well-respected American coaches, including Bernie Wagner, the Olympic coach, Dick Railsback, a former pole-vault champion and member of the Striders team, and Tim Vollmer, who was assigned to be in charge of the weight events. One of our top steeplechasers, Kelly Jensen, assisted me with distance runners. We would later be joined by our good friends from Reno, Bill Berrum, who would assist with the swimming program, and his wife Jackie. Andy Miller, the physical trainer from our Striders track team, and Joe Barry, who coached basketball, and his wife Marylou also joined our little group of American expats. Having their families with us brightened our outlook. As long as our assignment would only last one year, Joyce reluctantly agreed to the move.

Anyone who has moved to another country is probably familiar with the frustrations involved. A multitude of questions seem to appear during the middle of the night when one should be sleeping. After a long period of strained deliberation, we packed three large crates of items that we were sure would be essential. Once we arrived in Saudi Arabia, we unpacked only one of them. The two crates that remained unpacked proved that Americans, in their quest for comfort, often overestimate the amount of essential material things. The two crates contained clothing, shoes, cooking utensils, and books that proved to be anything but indispensable.

I had to leave early in order to help the Saudi track team prepare for a scheduled meet in Egypt, leaving Joyce in Agoura to handle the most difficult parts of the move. The stress of leaving our comfortable home and making travel arrangements for she and our two daughters took a toll on my wife. She had already arranged to stay with my mother in Seattle for a short vacation, but by that time, she was so exhausted that she passed out during her stay. A few days later, she continued on to London for another layover with our friends, Mark and Annette Winzenried, who were living there at the time. They assured Joyce that the Saudi experience would be an adventure that we would never forget. Thanks for the encouraging words, Mark, but stepping on the plane for the long trip to Riyadh almost caused Joyce to abandon the entire trip. It turned out to be an adventure that we will never forget!

My journey to Riyadh took place one month before my family arrived. I arrived at the airport alone and was immediately shocked by the stifling weather and exotic surroundings as soon as I stepped out of the plane. Of course, I had heard stories about the heat in the Saudi desert, but nothing could prepare you for the 115-degree oven. Even though it was 1975, Riyadh seemed like a scene from a Bible movie. Visiting Western businessmen could be seen scattered among Saudi men who wore long white robes and keffiyehs and ghutras wrapped around their heads. A number of women wearing traditional long robes (abayas) with their faces covered were mixed with the throng arriving from Western European destinations.

My Whittaker contact was nowhere to be seen. I was getting anxious and feared that there might have been some miscommunication regarding my arrival time. It was not a comfortable feeling being left on my own in a hot land where nobody understood English. I took a taxi to the only local hotel. Fortunately, I met an

American oil businessmen staying at the hotel who informed me that he, too, was waiting for Saudi officials to initiate contracts. He warned me that that Saudis were not concerned about time and he, also, had experienced the frustration of waiting for people to show up. If a Saudi happened to be in the desert working with his falcon during the time he had scheduled for a meeting, you could wait forever. It was a harbinger of things to come when dealing with Saudis. After waiting nearly two days without being contacted by Americans or Saudis, frustration set in. Finally, a smiling Whittaker contact appeared and, with no apologies, took me to our director's villa. It was my first encounter with what was probably the "Insha'Allah" custom: "if Allah wills it," I'll be there. As soon as I had unpacked my small suitcase, I was told that I would be traveling with the track team in a few days. Our first stop would be Basra, Iraq, followed by a flight to Cairo. Bernie Wagner felt uncomfortable with the itinerary, since my name would be the only non-Saudi name on the group's manifest. Because we didn't want to disappoint our hosts, we agreed to the conditions.

I barely had a chance to get to know my athletes or our group's leader, Nashat, an Egyptian coach who did not particularly like me or any of the Western coaches brought into the program. Nashat didn't want to lose his lucrative job, but nevertheless took every opportunity to show his disrespect for Americans. Upon arrival in the Basra airport, the officials checked off the names of our athletes on the travel manifest: Mohammed, Abdul, Ibrahim, etc. The last name that was read (at least it sounded familiar) was Petersons. After realizing that an American was on the list, they separated me from the group. Nashat was not at all upset and seemed content to ditch me there. An Iraqi official took my passport and led me to a cell where two terrified boys from Bangladesh were being held. I realized that I was not about to be invited to a friendly intercultural reception. Hours passed without being contacted by an official to whom I could plead my case.

23. Pete with his Saudi driver in front of Whittaker building in Riyadh, 1975.

One of the Bangladeshi men spoke some English and explained that they had been waiting days in our cell, and had been given little food. That was enough for me. I burst through the door of the office and demanded that they return my passport. I refused to leave, and eventually they put me on the next plane to Cairo. They probably realized that I wasn't about to hand over a "baksheesh" payment (bribe). An hour later, with my passport intact, I was put on a rickety old Aeroflot plane to Cairo.

From my early observation, it seemed that Cairo was a very large, overpopulated city with old and new mixed all together. Donkey carts shared the streets with new Mercedes Benz, both caught in the snarl of Cairo's traffic. Westerners shared the narrow streets with men dressed in their traditional robes. My hotel was situated on a street with twisted alleyways. Their narrow passageways were filled with stalls, boutiques, workshops; making and selling their tapestries, marble statues and foodstuffs. Across the way some men were enjoying their traditional water pipes, blowing smoke into the humid air. I only wish I felt good enough to record these memorable scenes with my Nikormat, later to be shown to my students.

The food on the flight was terrible, and I felt sick upon arrival in Cairo. Again, I faced the same difficulty of not knowing where to go, since neither Nashat nor anyone else from our team was anywhere to be seen. With frustration setting in once again, I asked the taxi driver to take me to the Hilton or Sheraton Hotel, where I could buy a meal. I had not eaten for nearly a day, and was starved for some Western food. However, the driver dumped me at a dilapidated hotel in the middle of the city and drove off before I could object.

Fatigue had set in, and after the airplane meal that featured suspicious pieces of lamb drowned in dark gravy, I barely made it up to my room. I cannot remember being this sick anytime in my life. I thought that perhaps a Coke might help, since I didn't trust the water. I called downstairs and was able to get a lady to bring me a bottle of Coke. Instead of handing me the Coke, she proceeded to taste it before handing me the bottle. I stayed in my shabby hotel for almost two days before calling the American Consulate. A young marine with a cheerful voice heard my plea for help but informed me that there was nothing he could do. He advised me to check the phone book and look for a doctor. Thanks a lot! I decided to leave the hotel as soon as possible and try again to locate the

Hilton or Sheraton on the Nile. Following what had to be the most appreciated meal of my life, a cheeseburger with a Coke, a hotel employee told me that an Egyptian by the name of Nashat was looking for me. And so began my job as a track coach in a Middle Eastern desert: an odyssey never to be forgotten.

My first track meet left me even more discouraged, if not depressed. Our athletes didn't have much talent, and they definitely lacked technique, not to mention endurance and competitive spirit. That's when I first realized that my American colleagues and I were in for a challenging task.

LIFE IN RIYADH

Riyadh, despite being stuck in the middle of an inhospitable desert, is a rapidly growing city. Its inhabitants must endure stifling temperatures and frequent windstorms. It is a city of extremes. We never got used to the pungent smell of the garbage that seemed to be piled everywhere. The long-tended fires burning in open fields and the spiced scent of lambs roasting on spits tested the strength of your stomach. It was difficult to miss the odors of stale sweat as men toiled in the oppressive heat. Most had not bathed in weeks. Men from Yemen and other nearby countries did most of the physical labor. It was difficult to find a building or villa because streets were mostly unnamed. From public address systems placed in minarets came the daily wailing call of people being summoned to worship, a universal sound in the Middle East. Goats wandered freely in their search for food, accompanied by attacking hordes of flies, which prompted some visitors to conclude that a swatting motion with your hands should be the official Saudi salute.

The Whittaker Corporation supplied housing to those of us in the coaching program. Our compound consisted of several villas and a swimming pool, all enclosed by an eight-foot wall. I know what you are thinking when we mention "our villa" with a private swimming pool: how can we complain about such luxury? One problem was that we had no chemicals to keep our pool water safe. In no time at all, the water turned milky green, transitioning eventually to a light brown. None of us wanted to look at it. Our air conditioning unit was placed too close to our front door, making it a hazard to be avoided with each entry or exit from the building. We had to remember to lower our heads as we entered our villa. If you didn't pay attention, a collision with your forehead was a certainty. Saudis did not save their garbage. Instead, they threw it over the walls for goats to consume. The structures were poorly built, so dust particles found their way through the numerous cracks and covered everything inside. Because of the frequent sandstorms, dust and grit seemed to be everywhere and in everything: hair, clothes, and even food. Puddles of water would pour through the doors and windows during the rainy season. The muddy roads made driving a challenge. In our villa, mud would seep through cracks and cover the floors. Electricity was usually available, but on an irregular schedule. Without warning, lights would go out for long periods. The lights would fluctuate from powerful surges of brightness to barely noticeable glowing filaments. Close to our "villa" was a minaret whose speakers blared out the call for prayers for the faithful five times a day. We didn't mind the intrusion so much as the scratchy sound of the worn-out disks they used. In order to curtail, or hopefully eliminate the trillions of flies, a novel plan was devised. Dozens of small planes flew over the city, one after another, back and forth, spraying insecticides. We were never warned, but after seeing the sticky stuff on our faces, hair, and hands, we didn't hesitate to run for cover. We were all concerned about the availability of medical care if the falling poisons or other environmental hazards caused anyone to get sick. Being un-fortunate in not knowing a Western doctor, Joyce and the girls had to trust a male Egyptian doctor, who spoke hardly any English. It was also highly improbable that such a doctor had any experience in treating women's health problems. The three-thousand-strong royal family (totaling nearly seven thousand today), on the other hand, had a state-of-the-art hospital, staffed with American, Swedish, and British doctors and nurses. The hospital was supported by the very same Whittaker Corporation that sponsored our program. On rare occasions, we were permitted to enter the hospital grounds, but forbidden to swim in their crystal-clear aqua-blue pool. It saddened Marni, standing by the beautiful pool, hoping to enjoy a swim.

Since Saudi Arabia sits on an aquifer as big as Oregon, there was more than an ample supply of water available. It was stored in huge mushroom-like towers throughout the city. We already knew that Saudis had large oil fields throughout the desert. There was a joke going around about Saudis expressing disappointment if they struck oil when drilling for water. Massive trucks delivered water on a weekly basis to our villa. It was emptied into wells that had been constructed below the compound. The same truck drivers also caused frequent power outages by ripping electric power lines to shreds as they drove wildly through construction zones. In order to maintain a steady supply of groceries, we had to take separate trips to the meat market, the vegetable stand, and other stores that sold sundry items. We found a store that sold ice cream, but we quickly lost our appetite when we noticed that it was located next to a foul-smelling sewage outlet. That made it easy to give up desserts.

It was natural to share both our joys and frustrations with the people who lived under the same conditions as we did. To some, the stresses of such a foreign lifestyle spawned understandable complaints and discontent. Gossip, which spread like wildfire, often created jealousy. Why is so-and-so getting more pay? Why is he being sent to Europe to purchase uniforms while I am stuck here? Why don't we have a driver like that other family? When new coaches and personnel arrived, everyone was eager to welcome them and make sure they were informed of the latest scuttlebutt. John

Second, our weight and fitness coach, regularly let us know how much he missed his dog, which he had to leave back in the States. The anguish he endured while considering all the options about having his dog sent from home created a stressful environment for everyone. Saudis viewed dogs as a nuisance, to be shot rather than treated as pets. The wild "salukis," as they were called, usually roamed in packs during the night, often attacking people. Early one morning as I was getting ready for a scouting trip to Jeddah, I had a narrow escape when a pack of ten to fifteen approached me as I was walking toward my Volkswagen. I was fortunately able to jump on top of the car and scare them off. Saudis went to extreme lengths to avoid being touched by dogs. With all of our shared frustrations, we eventually realized that it was up to all of us to make life within our group more bearable. After all, we came here to coach and develop programs that would enhance and energize sports in Saudi Arabia. Somehow, we had survived the first months intact, and the succeeding months passed by almost unnoticed.

Just when things started to go relatively smoothly, we were presented with some other unexpected hurdles. The Saudi princes were not so much interested in the athletic prowess of individual athletes, but rather in showing off the yet-to-be-built athletic facilities to other princes. Before we could accomplish our goal of improving sports facilities and acquiring equipment, we had to deal with the Saudi expectation of baksheesh for every financial transaction. Everyone wanted a cut of the action, which was "business as usual" throughout the Middle East. Even our own directors eventually learned the game. Here was the plan: request larger amounts of money than were needed and then bribe the US or European companies that produce the needed items by giving them baksheesh if they would list a higher figure on the invoice. After submitting them to the prince, the Saudi officials kept the difference. The middlemen made out like bandits. All of our companies learned that baksheesh was business as usual, so they might as well get used to it. Even our

Whittaker Corporation joined in the game, which explained why company officials were sent to the United States to purchase recreational vehicles for their recruitment excursions.

Remember my trip to Egypt with the Saudi team? I needed my passport for a flight in just a few days. (The Saudis automatically kept all passports upon entry into the country). Whittaker had to pay an extra one hundred dollars for a middleman in order to get the document within one day. In a week, the baksheesh was dropped to only twenty-five dollars.

Saudi track and field, as well as other sports, was in its infancy. The exception, of course, was soccer, the one sport that most youngsters were eager to play. We had to start from scratch. We were not only dealing with boys and men who had never trained, but they also had cultural beliefs that viewed sports differently than in the United States. Who, in their right mind, would go into the burning desert to run, throw, or jump? The belief that Allah decided their future carried a lot more weight than some Yankee coach urging them to run faster or jump higher. Whenever we tried to encourage them to run faster, their answer was often, "Insha'Allah," only if Allah was willing. One time, after an improved week of training, I told my top runner that he would win his race. He wagged his finger and shook his head from side to side. I knew that this would probably be his response even before I presented him with my little pep talk. I learned to find other ways to motivate, such as matching a younger and faster runner with an older, less talented runner, to see who could run a faster lap. Another technique to stimulate competition was to pit a Bedouin against a Wahhabi and let the grudges that had been brewing for centuries work their magic. With the arrival of Ramadan, one of two major religious observances, all training came to a stop. For an entire month, Saudis abstained from eating food during the daytime, although they were allowed to drink water. We had little choice but to schedule night training sessions. It was difficult to ask an athlete with a stomach full of food and water to run or jump. The other major religious observance was the Hajj, at which time the entire city seemed to shut down. The Hajj is a pilgrimage to the holy city of Mecca that is all but a requirement for any pious Muslim. There was little chance of enticing our athletes to train, since most of them simply disappeared.

During these idle times we visited marketplaces, or *souks*, for shopping. To many of us who had never experienced bargaining, a delightful thrill awaited us. We should have remembered our trips to Mexico, where we sometimes bargained with vendors. In Saudi Arabia, we learned to never agree on the price asked by a merchant. Shopkeepers and street vendors disliked it when inexperienced Westerners accepted an initial asking price. They wanted to have fun with you, so it was customary while shopping to point out imperfections on a rug, or the loose threads on a shirt, or even a color that seemed to have faded. Slowly, the price came down from 500 Riyals to 350, then to 280, and so on. To make sure that the bargaining continued, they offered sweet tea, always served extra hot. You and the merchant were really hitting it off now. Gold is priced at a set rate, so bargaining didn't help. While checking out a beautiful watch and inquiring about the price, I was surprised when the merchant told me to take it with me, wear it, and then come back for an agreed-upon price. Although he trusted me to bring it back, he knew magistrates who would track me down, just in case. You wouldn't want to risk it, considering the punishment that a thief might receive is the loss of his hand. I didn't feel like losing my hand, so I declined his kind offer. We bought some rugs and a beautiful gold neck chain that Joyce presented to me. I still wear it every day as a reminder of our visit to the gold market. We had a driver, so it was easy for us to travel to the city, but we made sure to avoid going during prayer times. No one could be unaware of when it was time for prayers. Five times each day, loud chants came from the speakers at the tops of minarets. The designated times for religious observances was strictly enforced. Saudi Arabia had no regular police force, but there were plenty of religious magistrates, who were dressed in typical Arab fashion but carried long sticks, urging people to pray while making sure that the stores were closed. One early visit to town, Joyce was approached by a magistrate who decided that she was improperly dressed. For her perceived transgression, she was surprised to hear a stream of Arabic anger and found the sidewalk in front of her struck repeatedly with a long stick and then spat upon. She quickly ducked into the nearest store and waited until our driver came by and picked her up. At this point she went to a tailor and had several long "thoubs" made, similar to a man's dress shirt reaching to the ankles. Another time, as we drove to the city and approached the main square, we saw a Ferris wheel and a merry-go-round. Our girls became excited and asked if they could ride them. We said, "What the heck? Let's let them have some fun." A sizeable crowd started to gather, which made Joyce and me uncomfortable. We didn't know why the crowd was shouting and angrily pointing at our daughters. Then it hit us: the crowd consisted of only men and boys; women or girls were nowhere to be seen. It was a stern reminder that only boys and men are allowed to ride Ferris wheels, go to soccer matches, or participate in any other type of public gathering. I attended a soccer match between the Saudi national team, coached by the famous Hungarian Puskás, and a small village team from Austria. There were over twenty thousand spectators, all males. The invincible Saudi team "crushed" the Austrian village team 2–"1 (officials had to make sure that the Saudis won if they wanted to avoid punishment from the princes). The next day's headline read, "Saudi team beats Austrian national team in an upset."

Being an avid amateur photographer, I sometimes carried my Nikon camera with me to record Saudi life. I quickly learned that most Saudis strenuously object to having their pictures taken. It is based on the principle that no human images should be duplicated, only floral or geometric designs. It explains why you will never see pictures of humans in their art, an attitude that Westerners who appreciate paintings inspired by Biblical events find difficult to understand. One evening we were driving on a desert road at sunset. We stopped the car so I could take a silhouette picture of a nomad by a fire, with the setting sun as a background. It was a scene out of *National Geographic,* but the nomad was apparently unappreciative of the attention he was receiving from me. He grabbed a section of two-by-four lumber, quickly rose from his seat, and threw the board at me. We drove off quickly before he could pick up his missile and come after us. After the nomad incident, I was cautious about photographing Saudis. On the other hand, we found that modern Saudis loved to have their pictures taken. Our athletes were eager to be photographed and loved to see the results. I imagine the scene today, with iPhones allowing anyone to record images discreetly. Today's technology would make it difficult for magistrates to enforce their edicts. I'm confident that it will totally change the Arab world, making young people able to break down communication barriers. One tenet of Saudi society that was frustrating for us was their fervent belief that "everyone is equal in the eyes of Allah" no matter what they were trying to accomplish. For example, if you are at the end of a long line, Allah wills it that you are equal to the person at the front. Standing in lines while waiting to purchase items often ended in frustration. People were always crowding in front of you or reaching over your shoulder to interrupt your transaction. Common courtesy and politeness were nonexistent: you had the right to push, shove, or interrupt the person in front of you in order to assert your right as his equal. Berny Wagner and the rest of our coaches wanted to fly to a city that had organized a track group near the city of Jeddah, the Saudi city on its west coast. We hoped to locate some new and talented athletes. We arrived at the airport and purchased our tickets early so we would be assured of seats on the plane. As we waited for the flight, we noticed that many others were arriving to purchase tickets for the same plane. The plane was ready to leave, so we moved toward the gate. All of a sudden, people started pushing and shoving, trying to get ahead of us. Tim Vollmer was at the front of our group and was in no mood for such behavior. With his patience and tolerance for Allah's "any way to be first" wishes exhausted, he grabbed people on each side of him, and pulling them emphatically to the rear of the line. He was the biggest and strongest man in the airport, so nobody quarreled with him. When we finally boarded our plane, we noticed that several passengers who had purchased tickets were left behind. They were simply out of luck, to which they probably rationalized as "Insha'Allah." Apparently, the Saudi airline, like many US airlines, had overbooked the flight.

Our Whittaker building was located on a roundabout street circle, so we had a good view of Saudi driving behavior and how they dealt with auto accidents. But first, it must be understood that Saudis are permitted to buy a car and drive it without a driver's license, or any proof that they can safely operate a vehicle. Since driving was a new experience for most Saudis, they found it perfectly acceptable to learn while driving. We noticed that their patience wore thin when cars ahead of them didn't start moving immediately after a light change. Their "weapon" was the horn, and how they loved to use it! The horns created a multi-pitched cacophony that was annoying and often nerve-racking. After an accident, crowds usually gathered quickly, and arguments seemed to involve not only the drivers, but everyone else close to the accident. The size of the group would depend on how well each driver pleaded his case to both the other driver and the surrounding crowd. After a considerable amount of time had passed, one group grew larger, and the support for that side's driver forced the other driver to concede and pay up. It was a raucous but practical way of determining which driver was at fault. No exchange of driver's licenses or insurance information was required. Even the religious magistrates stayed away. Money was exchanged, and everyone walked away satisfied. Americans who hired taxis that became involved in serious accidents were advised to pay quickly and disappear as fast as possible. Serious cases warranted drastic punishments. Also, we were warned by veteran Westerners not to be near the "chopping square" in the middle of the city on days when punishments were meted out. Religious magistrates gathered up people and made them watch the punishments, which included beheadings with a curved machete-type sword, whippings, and the cutting off of arms or hands. We heeded their advice and stayed away from the area. We had no desire to see barbaric punishments accompanied by loud shouts of approval from the onlookers.

This gives you a glimpse of how the swiftly Saudi justice system works. Saudis believe that by making everyone observe punishments, fewer people would be willing to violate the laws of the Koran.

Life went on, and we continued our attempt to develop a track-and-field program from scratch. We relished any success, no matter how small it seemed at the time. Joe Barry took over the basketball program, and Bill Berrum worked with their swimmers. Tim Volmer found some rusty Chinese barbells for weight training, Dick Railsback was able to put together enough stands for pole vaulting, and Berny Wagner began coaching sprinters. Andy Miller was available for physiotherapy, something totally alien to Saudis, but a big help for us. Kelly Jensen and I rounded up our distance runners and took them for runs around the stadium. Progress was always interrupted due to difficulties in communication. Even though we had interpreters, we found out that they had no background in or any idea about the events we were attempting to describe. Here is an example: I asked my Lebanese interpreter to explain to our runners how to run a certain distance. He turned to face them and proceeded with a lengthy description in Arabic, and then turned to look back at me. I asked him if he had explained what I told him to tell the runners. He gazed at me with a straight face and asked: "Tell them what?" So much for reliable interpreters. I felt confident, judging from previous successful encounters in Venezuela and Jamaica, that I would get the same results if the concept could be communicated properly. Communicating my Run for Fun philosophy was next to impossible in a country whose citizens are accustomed to avoiding strenuous movement. You can imagine how difficult it was to convince runners to enjoy the act of running in 115-degree heat. Every instinct told them to slow down and try not to work up a sweat. Kelly Jensen, my assistant from Oregon State, was a tremendous asset. He practically took them by their hands and with his diplomatic smile, urged them on. He is one of those rare Americans who could go anywhere around the globe and instantly fit in. His sense of humor and friendly smile helped lower the inherent suspicions of our athletes, eventually winning them over to our side. With both of us coaxing, we were able to communicate the need to complete a warm-up and stretching routine before they did a workout or ran a race. We were delighted to be able to convince them to sneak in a few more miles. Kelly was an outstanding steeplechaser at Oregon State, which gave him the idea of jumping over barriers set up around a stadium as part of their training. Other days we took them outside the city limit to run the sand dunes or through the nearby palm-lined valleys. They started to enjoy the longer runs while being entertained with Kelly's funny facial gestures or my crazy antics. They certainly didn't want to miss out on "Pete and Kelly" concerts when we did our best to imitate Western pop singers. Both of us were delighted when they showed up more regularly. Numbers increased, both in participation and in miles covered. One of their favorite amusements was watching Kelly and me imitating their running styles. Eventually, they followed us without being prodded. Kelly felt that it was time to introduce other strategies. We drove them out to the desert to a point far enough so they had no choice but to run back. They even trusted Kelly when he risked taking them out in the desert when it looked as if there was an approaching windstorm. On one of their long runs, a sandstorm overtook them, forcing the athletes to lie flat on the ground, cover their faces, and wait for the winds to subside. Other times we challenged them to stay up with us in sprints. I worked with interval training routines and announced times so runners could judge a pace. Eventually, an all-weather track was built, which made training much easier. It didn't take long to discover that we were working with less talented athletes than we had hoped. If these were the best runners the Saudis could assemble, we couldn't expect miracles. We were surprised to learn that many of our athletes were recruited from national and royal guard units, and with the help of guaranteed bonuses, were enticed to "become athletes for the Americans."

There were many frustrations during our Saudi experience, but our biggest disappointment was not being able, for a variety of reasons, to develop the type of athletic program that we had originally envisioned. I wanted our top distance runners to have the opportunity to experience competition in an international setting. I arranged a cross-country race in Brussels, Belgium, during the winter, although it turned out to be more of a local competition. My shadow, Nashat, was appointed the official representative of our group and, most importantly, the person in control of our funds. Knowing him, we were all sure that he made arrangements to receive more than ample funds. I noticed that he carried a briefcase full of traveler's checks. Later, I found out that he was prepared to bribe local officials and runners so that our competitors were allowed to finish near the front of each race. If our runners were successful, Nashat would receive a handsome bonus from the prince. He failed to see the absurdity of asking dozens of local runners to hold back and let the Saudis finish near the front. After all, Allah would wish it so. In another instance, the basketball coach who replaced Joe Barry thought his players would fare well against a relatively weak team from Mozambique. After his team lost to the Africans, Saudi pride was damaged. Upon returning to Riyadh, the coach was given twenty-four hours to leave the country.

Following a few months of steady improvement, we arranged a trip to Switzerland for additional international competitions and the opportunity to train at the fabulous Swiss National Sports Training Center in Magglingen (Macolin in French), overlooking scenic Lake Biel. We knew that this experience would be an eye-opener for them. The spacious grounds, surrounded by mountains, had tree-lined trails radiating in all directions. It offered both an outdoor track facility as well as an indoor hall for weight training, volleyball, basketball, tennis, and swimming. During one training session in this beautiful setting, we were joined by athletes from other countries, including the legendary Belgian Olympian, Ivo Van Damme. We noticed that our sprinters had joined some athletes from other countries for a few wind sprints. One of the young ladies immediately stood out with her flawless running technique. Later, we learned that she was the Israeli national champion, and she seemed unconcerned about sharing a track with Arabs. Had our prince found out, it could have been the end of our jobs. We had another treat planned for them. We knew that our Saudis had never been to an alpine setting and had never touched snow. Since we were so close to the Alps, we decided to arrange a train ride up to famous Mount Eiger. The mountains were still packed with ice and snow, and we knew that our athletes would be inspired by the spectacular scenery.

Leaving Interlaken, a beautiful city located between two deep-blue lakes, we traveled by train to Grindelwald, considered to be one of the gems of the Alps, with expensive hotels set in idyllic alpine scenery. We joined busloads of tourists from all over the world, especially Japan. From Grindelwald, our train took us to the main station, where we changed to a cogwheel train. We inched our way up the mountain, occasionally looking back to see the chalets of Grindelwald becoming smaller and smaller. The Saudis stared in amazement as we approached the massive face of Eiger. Our athletes were aware that many climbers who had dared to challenge the rocky slopes never made it back. As we climbed higher, we noticed that the breathtaking views had seemed to put our Saudi runners into a trance. Their faces revealed a mixture of fear and wonder as they dared each other to look out the window. After a final exchange of cars, we were lifted to the top of Jungfrau, which, at 13,000 feet, is the highest railway station in Europe. This was their first opportunity to touch snow, and they were instantly transformed by the experience. They reacted much as a child would, rolling joyously in the powder and laughing. We didn't understand what they were saying, but seeing them so happy was equally rewarding for us. Their antics revealed an innocent joy seldom seen from stoic Saudi males. We left feeling confident that they looked forward to sharing tales of their alpine adventures with friends back in the sands of Arabia.

Having Joyce, Marni (9), and Corey (2) with us gave us all a chance to be back in Europe and enjoy some delicious meals. It had been a long time since we had been able to drink real milk and eat salads that didn't have to be dipped in Clorox water before being eaten. On one occasion, Joyce and the girls found themselves stranded near Lake Biel. Joyce was fortunate to meet a lovely Swiss woman named Arlette and her two daughters. Arlette kindly offered to take Joyce and the girls back to the hotel. That chance encounter was the beginning of a lifelong friendship between our families. Since our first meeting in 1976, we have visited Emil and Arlette in Biel on other occasions. We always enjoyed their fondue

Riyadh's new stadium : Saudi vs. small village Austrian team

Saudi team competing in Damascus: Kelly kneeling in front row

and having Emil as an enthusiastic tour guide for drives through the countryside.

Other members of our group in Riyadh were able to travel to Sri Lanka and sometimes Kashmir, mainly to purchase prized rugs. Most of those who remained in Riyadh just wanted to escape the stifling heat. Our director, Glenn Randall, was a connoisseur of exotic tapestries. For a lover of fine weavings, a trip to Kashmir was like a trip to Mecca. He planned to purchase expensive rugs, which he hoped to ship to the United States and sell for a handsome profit. The trick was getting the weavings out of Saudi Arabia. He eventually found a way to include them in the equipment plane that was flying to the Montreal Olympics.

Life became more bearable after Joyce found an international school for Marni and a teaching job for herself. We met an American oil executive who invited us to his comfortable villa to watch the latest movies from the states. Marni and Corey were delighted when he surprised them by making popcorn, which was followed by real ice cream that had been purchased from the company's commissary. Chitty Chitty Bang Bang was the girls' favorite movie to watch. These American workers had become so accustomed to their lifestyle of plenty that they barely missed the States. When they did manage to return, they even experienced a degree of a culture shock when they saw how drastically things had changed. The petro-executives enjoyed high salaries (much of which was tax-exempt), generous fringe benefits, fresh food from the commissary, feature movies from the States, and frequent all-expenses-paid trips to Europe for vacation and R & R. They had plenty of reasons to remain in Saudi Arabia.

GETTING READY FOR THE MONTREAL OLYMPICS

Despite the lack of equipment, constant interruptions, barriers in communication, and cultural misunderstandings between athletes and Saudi administrators and princes, we felt that we had made reasonable progress. Untrustworthy Egyptian officials like Nashat continued to be more of a hindrance than a help, but we were pleased that our athletes were getting in better shape and were refining their vaulting and jumping techniques. Tim Volmer discovered a number of weight-event prospects, and with the help of his assertive personality and strong leadership, they made impressive gains. Kelly and I noticed that our runners were recording faster times and even taking on a little of the Run for Fun philosophy that we tried to instill. With progress on multiple fronts buoying our spirits, we arranged a meet with Syrian runners in Damascus. Although the Saudis' confidence grew when they defeated the Syrians, they still lacked the talent to be creditable Olympic caliber performers. It was, however, a start that eventually led to impressive performances.

A decision was made by the International Olympic Committee to invite, for the first time, Saudi athletes to the Olympics. We were elated, since it would erase any suspicions that our efforts had been a waste. To us, it was important that our athletes be exposed to the world outside of the Middle East and given a chance to experience higher levels of competition. The seeds were planted, and we had confidence that in a number of years the country could produce some athletes who were potential medalists. I'm sure Kelly influenced the Saudi steeplechaser who later won the bronze medal in the world championships. The sports establishment took notice when a Saudi long jumper exceeded twenty-eight feet in some international meets. Dick Railsback's jumpers made additional impressive gains after his second year in Riyadh.

Two women (Sara and Vojda) received a standing ovation when they were introduced at London in 2012 as the first Saudi female competitors in an Olympic Games. Unfortunately, they received no ovations when they returned to their home country. They were reviled by many and even called prostitutes, since the Koran forbade such women's activities. One step forward and two steps back.

SAUDI ARABIA TODAY

Although we might not recognize much of it, Joyce and I wonder what it would be like to revisit Riyadh today. As it has all over the world, it would stand to reason that global economics and technology have challenged their traditions. Just as the neighboring kingdoms have modernized their countries with construction, reclamation of land, installation of sea-water desalinization plants, as well as engaging in competition to see which country can claim possession of the world's tallest structure, Saudi Arabia is not far behind. They have huge reserves of oil, which serves to push their rulers in two directions. They want to guide their country into the modern age, which sometimes conflicts with their deeply held belief that Saudi traditions should be honored. We have seen many pictures of impressive buildings in Riyadh that did not exist in 1976, but at the same time, we have read accounts that describe a way of life that seems unchanged from when we lived there in the 1970s. Women are still unable to drive, unless they do so inside the protective walls of their palatial villas, but many dare to drive anyway. There are still no movie theaters and few sports for women. Tourists are now allowed to visit the country, so they might be advised to study up on Saudi customs and Islamic laws. Overuse of camera phones can get you in big trouble, and alcohol is still strictly forbidden (at least in public). There are Starbucks, Saks Fifth Avenue, Baskin Robbins, and huge shopping malls where people can socialize and escape the oppressive heat. Not long ago, women could gather in their homes to debate and discuss political and social issues. Today, the government needs to grant permission for such gatherings. The king has allocated $32 billion for education-related projects, especially sciences, along with generous allowances for students wishing to study outside Saudi Arabia. The number of Saudi students in the United States has risen to nearly forty-five thousand, a number exceeded only by China, India, and South Korea. My

Alma Matter, USC, has one of the fastest-growing populations of Middle Eastern graduate students in the United States. It's not uncommon to see Saudi students watching Trojan football teams and flashing the Trojan victory sign.

LEAVING SAUDI ARABIA:
MONTREAL OLYMPICS (1976)

We were elated to return to Europe before the Montreal Olympics. Joyce was fortunate to be able to stay with our dear friends outside London and watch the Olympics on advertisement-free BBC. I accompanied the Saudi team to Montreal and continued to coach our athletes. I informed my directors that, due to my job back in Agoura, I would terminate my present coaching job. I told them that I did not have tenure in my school district, so it became imperative that I return. The directors tried to convince me to stay, but a year in Saudi Arabia was sufficient. The salary that we received from the Whittaker Corporation was not the same as originally promised. Because company officials seemed to have no clear plan for us, and our medical help was nowhere near what we had been promised, we found it easy to terminate our contract and return to the United States once the Olympics were complete.

24. Adidas or Puma, which way do I go?
Herzogenaurach, Germany, 1976.

We certainly do not regret our decision to spend a year out of our lives in such an unusual environment. We have more memories from that one year than from any other time period. I can still picture my inept interpreter from Jordan asking me, "Tell them what?" And the elder Saudi sitting by a fire in the desert and chasing me away for taking his picture. I'll always have the joyful memory of Saudis behaving like children, throwing snowballs at each other on top of Mount Eiger. I still have fond memories of Kelly Jensen showing Saudis that is possible to laugh while running through the burning desert. We still get together and correspond with Bill and Jackie from Reno, Andy Miller from New Jersey, Joe and Mary Lu from Ohio, and Dick Railsback from

Nebraska. I'm happy for Kelly Jensen, who is still coaching and recently attended his son's graduation from college. Our conversations seem to last forever, since we have so many experiences to relive, both the good and the ugly. Recently Joyce replayed a recorded message that she sent home during Christmas in 1976, crying, laughing, pausing frequently, and wiping away tears. Dean Martin's song, "Memories Are Made of This," fits the description perfectly.

LIFE IN SAUDI ARABIA – A WOMANS VIEW, by Joyce Petersons, Agoura, California

Forty years ago, in 1975, the fortunes of the Petersons family turned a sharp corner when we moved from Southern California to Saudi Arabia. Bill Toomey, gold medal winner in the '68 Mexico Olympic Games decathlon, connected my husband Pete with the Whittaker Corporation (famous for hospitals and yachts) who needed a track coach to help prepare a Saudi Arabian team to compete in the Montreal Olympic Games coming up in 1976.

Pete had to leave in September, so I proceeded to rent our house and pack up our belongings. The girls, Marni (8 years old) and Corey (15 months old), and I flew up to Seattle to spend a week with 'Omi', Pete's mother, and then we flew to England where Pete could meet us. Together we flew down into the heart of Saudi Arabia, into another time and space.

Life in Riyadh, the capitol of Saudi Arabia, began for us in a "four-villa" compound, meaning four separate houses with a swimming pool in the middle and a twelve foot wall surrounding us. We had a one story, two bedroom, newly built house with basic furniture, no carpets on the gritty cement floors and no coverings on any windows. We had landed at night, so there was nothing to do but make the beds, cover the windows with aluminum foil, and go to sleep. The following days our belongings arrived from the States, we went on a trip to a carpet shop downtown, and with that our first experience with prayers which stopped daily life five times a day. *Shops were closed suddenly and in the panic, I left my purse that first time. Luckily our driver was able to go back and retrieve it for me.*

Marni entered the 2nd grade in the International School with Mrs. Mary Lou Barry as her teacher. Mary Lou was Joe Barry's wife; he was one of the basketball coaches whom we met as neighbors in our four-villa first home. Marni loved going to school and enjoyed playing with Mrs. Barry's daughter Barbie after they were driven home by our Yemenese driver each day. Unfortunately our swimming pool was never cared for, so it quickly became unusable. In order to keep the mosquito population down, we took turns spraying the stagnating water with Raid every few days.

Patterns of life gradually developed in those first few months. The weather was much like Southern California – warm clear days and nights cooling down. Water was delivered twice a week by large water trucks whose drivers threw great long hoses over the outer wall into a hollow tank beneath the ground...water for everyone's use in cleaning and bathing. Drinking water was delivered in large Pepsi plastic containers. When the rains came, the doors swelled and water poured in under them along with large black water beetles! We would rush to grab several large bath towels to stop the rain from coming in under the windows of each room. Electricity would go off periodically (almost daily) leaving light bulb filaments glowing and refrigerators beginning to warm up.

Western doctors were unavailable to us Whittaker folk, so we had to find local doctors in time of need. Our baby Corey, still wearing diapers at this point, developed diaper rashes because we often could not get hot water to sanitize them. It wasn't long before we were forced to buy paper diapers – extremely expensive as a Western imported product. I found an Egyptian doctor in town and made an appointment to see him for Corey's bleeding rash and my own yeast infection. Men being first to get treated left us sitting in the women's waiting room with several *other women and their children. They kindly motioned for me to go in when the men's waiting room emptied. The doctor had me lie on his vinyl covered table to examine me. There was no paper to give his patients a sanitary place on which to lie. And then he placed Corey on the same spot where I had been examined! I quietly told myself we would both go into a warm sudsy bath when we got back home to our villa. As we left his office, the doctor handed me a prescription for penicillin – no amounts given as a dosage for me or Corey? "Just give her a smaller amount with her juice", he directed. Oh, my!!*

Shopping was an adventure. We would be picked up by our driver and taken into town, about ten minutes away. There was a small market where we could find paper diapers, Babybel cheese balls wrapped in red cellophane (great for pizza!), chocolate chips on a lucky day, and flour with which to make the pizza crust and cookies and pancakes, but we had to sift the tiny black bugs out of the flour several times before accepting the rest as "a little protein" in our baked products. Fresh produce could be found in a separate market but it had to be sterilized. One strong memory was receiving a birthday gift from one of our villa neighbors of washed, (Cloroxed!) lettuce leaves. It was the first salad I had had in several months.

Meat was sold on the streets, great slabs hanging, covered with flies, and roasting spits of camel meat filling the air with roasted meat odors mingled with raw sewage smells coming from open holes in the nearby sidewalks, often with men going in and out doing their required duties to keep the sewage flowing.

There was a stationery store that held some books, some writing supplies, and a few paintings. We were lucky to buy one, a treasure hanging in our living room forty years later! It is a large painting of a camel with two turbaned people, one riding and the other leading the camel through the arid desert – reminiscent of Biblical stories we had read as children.

The spring brought some changes. The Barry's left for home in Ohio and Marni now had a new 2nd grade teacher. We were moved from our four-villa to a brand new eight-villa – this one with a swimming pool that was well-cared for by a few local boys who hung out nearby, delightedly watching as we women in our bikinis played with their children in the pool. I was finally able to get a part-time job at the International School teaching music to all the elementary grades – K-6. I hadn't brought my teaching credential, but was accepted as a bona fide teacher and proceeded to plan lessons with songs and simple instruments for each grade level. At one point we were able to invite parents to come to a concert we put on in the central play yard. Everyone was quite satisfied with their accomplishments. I was grateful for the chance to make it happen.

Exploring the gold souk was a special event. Gold jewelry came in from India at a very reasonable price. We watched a black-robed Arab woman buy a gold bracelet that day. Her hand was covered with a rubber glove which was covered with Vaseline, so that the vendor could push a narrow gold bracelet onto her wrist which already had at least a dozen golden circlets on it. It seems a woman gets a new bracelet to commemorate each special birthday, anniversary, birth of a child, or other important event in her life. In other visits to the local souk, we found a lovely backgammon set made of detailed inlaid wood, a solid wooden trunk with detailed hammered brass plates lining the front, plus a few brass camels and a brass coffee pot. Pete got a neck chain which he still wears and enjoys, and I got a belly chain which was very popular back then.

Arab punishment is immediate and cruel – an eye for an eye. We were warned to do no shopping on Fridays as on that day each week, the religious magistrates (police) would round up everyone who was shopping in town and bring them to a central plaza where punishment was meted out according to the crime. A peeping Tom had an eye gouged out, a thief lost a hand to the ax, and a more serious crime resulted in beheading – all in front of the crowd who had been corralled into the square. The message was clear – this could happen to YOU! Follow the laws of the land! We studiously avoided going into town on Fridays.

The world outside the walls of our homes and villas in Riyadh was wild arid land. Out there in the desert roamed herds of goats who lived on the garbage flung over the walls by the locals. Also gangs of wild dogs desperately searched for food. They were called salukis and looked like whippets or greyhounds. Some of our American friends wanted to domesticate one, but it proved difficult. Saudi Arabians disapproved having dogs as pets. There were planes which periodically flew over the outskirts of town and dropped pesticide to keep mosquitoes and other insects from taking over. The same planes also flew over the town late at night shooting the salukis to keep their population down. One morning Pete had to go out early for a track and field meeting. He went through the gate in our wall and found himself surrounded by a pack of salukis barking and growling ferociously at him. He luckily managed to climb on top of his car and screamed and yelled at them. They backed off enough for him to jump down and climb into his car. Scary moments!

We were fortunate to make friends with an American family who worked in Riyadh for Chevron Oil Company. They often invited us on a Friday evening for a ham dinner, a movie with fresh popcorn, and even a beer or glass of wine. All of these treats were unavailable to us as the Whittaker 'honchos' separated themselves from the athletic coaches' families. Another special event was to be invited to a British household only to find a real pub...a large room furnished with a tall wooden bar complete with brass railing and several bar stools. Neon lights lit up the place and authentic liquor bottles lined the shelves. Back in the kitchen lived "Mother", the distillery that created 'sadiki', 200% pure alcohol made from sugar. They cut this with distilled water and imported flavors to make bourbon, gin, and vodka. If someone knocked at the door, one person would call out, "Is Mother home?" and someone else would answer, "Sorry, she is out right now". This was code for "Close the cabinets in the kitchen. A stranger is here." Of course, it was illegal to make booze in this Arab world of princes and kings. Who knows what the punishment would be?

Living in a foreign land has its ups and downs. One of the most difficult parts of life in Saudi Arabia for me was the lack of communication with family and friends at home. With no phones or computers at hand, we had to rely on snail mail which truly lived up to its name for us. We once sent a Christmas card to a friend and it took nearly a year to get to its destination! A few times we put together a cassette tape with all of our voices on it and sent it home to be shared with mothers and brothers and sisters. Months passed before we received any word that these tapes had reached their destination. These long waits made hearing that we would be leaving Saudi with the athletes in June a welcome reprieve.

Leaving Saudi Arabia in June of 1976 involved taking our family to Switzerland where the young team was given the opportunity to become accustomed to function in the Western world. We kissed the green ground when we landed in Zurich. We first lived in a small town Erlach, at the southern end of Lake Biel. The athletes and coaches spent their days training up in Magglingen, an amazing training camp up in the mountains above Biel. After a few weeks we were moved into a Swiss hotel in Biel. While there, the Arab boys had to learn to eat with knife and fork and to use a toilet properly. The maids refused to clean up after them as they were used to standing up over a hole instead of sitting down! One day the girls and I took a train and a ferry to get back to Erlach to pick up some photos from a local drugstore. Because it was so very warm, I left Marni with her sister for fifteen minutes in a cool café with a cold drink and a snack. Returning back at a run with our photos, I found they had been befriended by a Swiss lady, Arlette Gehrig. Thanks to her, the girls were safe and happy. After nearly forty years, Arlette and Emil, her husband, and their two daughters, Michelle and Pascal, have become like family in our relationship with each other.

Before the team left for Montreal, we met up with Jackie Berrum and their two girls, Kimberly and Samantha. Bill, one of the swimming coaches, and Pete traveled to Montreal while Jackie and I and our girls traveled from Switzerland to England. We had a great time jumping on trains with our luggage, flattening pennies under the train wheels with the girls and visiting friends and relatives along the way. We were lucky to watch the Olympic Games on TV in England with good friends, Ron and Jean Pickering. Ron had been an Olympic coach of Mary Rand Toomey, as well as a broadcaster with the BBC for track and field events. It was wonderful to watch the Olympic Games without commercials!

Returning home was amazing. Our beautiful home in Agoura was such a delight to return to. Pete resumed his wonderful job teaching at Agoura High School and Marni returned to our neighborhood elementary school for third grade. After being in school for a couple weeks, she shared with us that she realized it was an incredible experience living in such a different culture for a year, and experiencing Europe at such a young age. I believe it opened her eyes to live her life with a more open perception towards people and the world we live in.

BACK HOME IN AGOURA (1976)

There is nothing like coming home after spending a year in a strange country, away from friendly and familiar surroundings. We looked forward to enjoying, once again, the comforts of home, getting a good night's sleep in our own bed, eating fresh fruit and vegetables, drinking real milk, and being able to eat home-cooked meals. We missed our seasonal traditions, such as watching USC and UCLA fighting it out in the Coliseum or seeing the new fall TV shows.

We definitely wouldn't miss washing salads in Clorox or constantly wiping away fine sand from our floors and furniture. We were thankful not to have to walk on sidewalks with open sewers or listen to the scratchy recordings of the call to prayer that blared daily from the minarets. And above all, we would no longer have a need for *Insha'Allah, souks, or baksheesh.*

Agoura students welcomed me back warmly, eager to hear our stories about life in Saudi Arabia and the Montreal Olympics. I had amassed lots of pictures with my Nikon camera and was able to share them with my students. I made an agreement with them. Based on their productivity in world history, American government and public speaking classes during the week, I agreed to show my slides on Fridays. My strategy worked to perfection when I added information and firsthand observations that were part of the required curriculum. The students and I felt that my presentations were more relevant, visual, and immediate. Joyce was able to get a job as a music teacher at nearby Calabasas High School. She eventually joined me at Agoura, and we were thankful to the Las Virgenes school district for allowing such an arrangement. Even though it was unusual to have husband and wife teaching in the same school, it caused no inconveniences and everyone accepted "Mr. Pete" and "Mrs. Pete" to the faculty. In addition, both Marni and Corey were allowed to have us as teachers when they were at Agoura High School.

I was eager to get back to full engagement with my students. My goal was to approach everything with zest and vigor. I wanted to continue where I left off, trying to make a difference in students' understanding of historic and current topics. That meant a total immersion utilizing a variety of methods, and challenging my students by engaging them in their own, student-centered learning situations. I created my own lessons, utilized new teaching strategies, provided audiovisual materials, and invited interesting guest speakers for added enrichment. One of my students in economics knew Mr. Peterson (no relation), who owned classic cars and published several outdoor magazines. He brought with him at least one hundred magazines and pictures of his car collection. Students loved him because he shared so much of his personal background, inspiring many students to investigate new careers. Another guest speaker, a genius innovator in electronics from Hughes Research Lab in Malibu, told students how he helped develop the machines that scan price codes on retail goods. He did a wonderful job, so I asked him if he could repeat the presentation for another class. He replied, "No, thanks, one period already tired me out." I went on to teach four more classes that day.

I learned that students retain only 5 percent from lectures, unless you happen to be a super creative, interesting, and animated individual who is able to explore a topic that students find relevant to their lives. Very few of us fit that category. As a result, I kept my so-called lectures to a minimum and prepared a wide variety of background materials: selected handouts, visual presentations, case studies involving critical thinking, and student-generated research. Students called me "Mr. DVD" for finding interesting and applicable short selections to help them visualize the lesson content. We had twelve to fifteen mock trials of controversial historical figures, ranging from Joan of Arc to Heinrich Himmler (in absentia), Oliver North, Napoleon (in *Animal Farm*, by Orwell), General Sherman, and others. For additional learning activities, I found role-playing simulations to be effective as well, such as in creating a bill in Congress or experiencing the life of a Great Plains farmer in the 1800s. Perhaps the most important activity was essay writing. Students demonstrated their comprehension of the subject concepts through their essays. There was resistance at first, but once they grasped the importance of creating a persuasive essay and were able to acquire the necessary skills, students preferred essays to multiple-choice exams. For me, it required spending many extra hours and weekends reading student work, but it was important to track the developing powers of reasoning and self-discovery that were revealed by their responses. Both Joyce and I felt strongly that if students spent time writing essays, then we owed it to them to read them. It is still uplifting to read old student essays that I have kept in boxes in our garage. It was not unusual for us to take student essays with us whether we were on a trip or staying home on Saturdays and Sundays. I realize how fortunate I was during all my years as an educator to have the freedom to develop my own teaching style. Today it would be next to impossible to utilize the large number of critical-thinking lessons that I had created. Today's teachers are faced with strict guidelines for "covering the material," which is invariably followed by extensive multiple-choice testing in place of essays. It is demoralizing to read about public discontent with teachers and the continued threats of losing one's job. We hear the proclamation that "Anyone can teach." That might explain why some districts are hiring graduate students, many of whom have no teaching experience or formal training in teaching methods.

One of the classes that I requested to add to our curriculum was public speaking. I found that my students had poor speaking habits. Many sentences in students' everyday speech seemed to contain crutch phrases such as, "You know...Like, Yeah, Like...Aaah." These same phrases turned up regularly in their speeches. Others in our school, especially English teachers, felt the same, admitting that they had to lower scores due to student inability to communicate effectively. I wrote the speech course study and Las Virgenes Schools accepted it as a part of their secondary curriculum. I was off to the races. One of my first classes contained forty students from all grade levels, from freshmen to seniors. I created a demanding curriculum based upon my speech classes at USC. The age or class of a student didn't seem to matter, the speech program turned out to be a big success. On many occasions, my freshmen performed even better than the supposedly sophisticated seniors.

On the first day of class, one of my favorite strategies was to ask the new students to speak for a few minutes. I started the class by assigning a topic and having them discuss it informally. After a few minutes, the students switched partners and continued the discussion. This served as an icebreaker and seemed to reduce the understandable anxiety of speaking in front of strangers. During this time, I had hidden my video camera and had it running as each student presented an introductory talk. During the course of the semester, students learned to follow the class guideline that emphasized positive feedback during all evaluations of speeches. They accepted the premise that peer reviews of presentations must concentrate on how improvement can be made rather than downgrading the presenter. Students gradually became comfortable with the setting and overcame their initial shyness. At the end of the semester I announced, to their horror that I was going to play back the tapes of their initial speeches. They pleaded with me to skip over their speeches, remembering how badly they had gone.

Sometimes my retort to those who were not prepared earned the comment, "That's the way it crumbles, cookie-wise." In the end, however, they took pride in their ability to communicate ideas effectively and admitted that public speaking was one of their favorite and most useful classes.

25. Pete teaching a government class at Agoura High School, 1977.

GRENADA AND JAMAICA (1977; 1980)

GRENADA 1977

As a result of Bill Toomey's performance in the Mexico Olympics, many officials from foreign associations or heads of state asked him, as an official representative of the United States, to make an appearance as a guest coach. President Reagan sent him to the Munich Olympics as his representative of the United States and later appointed him to the President's Council for Fitness. I was honored when he arranged for my family and me to travel to the island of Grenada for a series of coaching clinics organized through the OAS (Organization of American States).

Although the island is approximately the size of Lake Tahoe, the presence of Joyce and the girls made the trip much more enjoyable. My assignment required traveling to various schools to promote physical fitness and coach young runners. After settling my family into the beachfront Holiday Inn hotel, which offered breathtaking views of the clear waters, I was able to carry out my assignments comforted in the knowledge that Joyce, Marni, and Corey were well taken care of. I was the only American coach on the premises, but we shared space with eight hundred American students attending the nearby medical school. As a working coach, I was not housed in the Holiday Inn but lived in a hut that provided comfortable but considerably more basic and crowded lodging. Even though Grenada was undergoing political turmoil, I and the other Americans in our compound always felt safe.

I was provided with a jeep driver who took me to schools throughout this small country. Grenadian children were happy to see an "Americano" and delighted to participate in relays, calisthenics, negotiating "par-course" exercise stations, and working as teams.

I remember how Bud Winters achieved so much with his enthusiasm for doing the little things well and allowing the participants to improve their fitness while having fun. I used the same approach and found that it worked. Spending almost two hours twice a day at each school was taxing, especially with the intense heat and humidity. The school sessions with local youth were followed by late-afternoon coaching clinics with the country's best athletes. Grenada is blessed with many healthy, talented, and coachable young people. Kirani James, Grenada's top 400-meter runner, recently won a gold medal in the London Olympics. However, a major barrier to success lies in the high unemployment rate of its young males. Grenada was founded by slaves and remained under British rule for many years. A positive legacy of its colonial history is a British-model school system that has produced a literacy rate of 90 percent. So far, that impressive literacy rate has not resulted in aggressive promotion of tourism or trade. Even though the island's best-known exports are spices, their production employs only a fraction of the population. Poverty has continued to make Grenada a struggling developing nation.

For the next few weeks, we were moved to smaller huts next to the hotel and close to the American medical school. Our new accommodations were more crowded, but we were able to go to some nice local restaurants, see parts of the island that we had not visited, and learn how spices were harvested and dried. On our beach walks, we met the famous British actor, Peter Ustinov. He was open and friendly, and we enjoyed comparing travel experiences. He was especially excited about his excursions to India. Years later, he included Bill Toomey in one of his adventure films. Some days we would venture out to the narrowest part of the island, which separated a glistening white sand beach on one side of the isthmus from a black sand beach on the other.

Many of us remember the rebellion that sprang up on the island in 1983, when a Marxist rebel takeover threatened the safety of nearly eight hundred American students attending St. George's Medical School. President Reagan ordered an invasion of Grenada to quell the uprising and to move our students to safety. It became known as the "Little War" and, by many critics, an unnecessary and somewhat comical invasion. Our ground forces had no official maps, so they relied on tourist maps. Artillery barrages from our naval ships hit the wrong targets, including a mental hospital and some of our own troops. Communications were totally uncoordinated between the ships and the troops on the island. Calls had to be made back to the United States on private phones and then relayed back to the ships, since no channels of communication had been established ahead of time. When asked about their safety, over 90 percent of the medical students felt that they were totally safe and did not want to be removed. In 1986, Clint Eastwood made a film called *Heartbreak Ridge,* with many of the parts acted out by US military personnel. The film is a fictional account of the real life invasion of Grenada by the USA, though some of the sequences in the movie are based on actual events from that engagement.

Joyce, Marni, and Corey had to leave after six weeks, leaving me another six weeks to complete my assignment. While on our isolated island, we missed hearing news from home and the latest world events. I longed for any news from America, but was lucky to find a BBC broadcast each evening at 6:00 p.m. My most vivid memory was the announcement of the passing of Elvis Presley. I can tell you the exact time in the late afternoon when BBC broadcasts were beamed while I was preparing my evening meal. It was sad to hear his songs repeated over and over again. Now I wish I could return to this special place and revisit some of the highlights with my grown-up family. One of our favorite pictures is that of Marni and Corey sitting on a donkey on the beach.

26. Corey and Marni on Grand Anse Beach in Grenada, 1977.

JAMAICA 1980

"Welcome to Jamaica" was Mark Winzenried's greeting to our family after we had arrived from the United States. Once again, we were able to take advantage of my coaching background and spend part of two summers in a beautiful tropical setting while coaching athletes. Mark operated a small vacation lodge that provided housing for visiting American athletes. Most of the guests were high-school runners who, like us, were enjoying a great summer escape while getting expert coaching from me, Brooks Johnson, and his wife, Dede. Mark had arranged for us to stay in Turtle Bay Towers in Ocho Rios, which is on the tourist side of the island. He was no stranger to Jamaica, having organized various musical events, including some performances by the legendary Bob Marley.

Coaching the Jamaican runners was a dream experience. They were eager to experiment with different approaches to training, including my Run for Fun methods along with the Johnsons' advice on sprinting. It was also valuable for me to learn sprinting drills that I could include in my training sessions. My hope was that improved sprinting techniques would be useful in developing better finishing kicks for my distance runners. Brian Diemer of Michigan, who later became America's top steeplechaser, was one such runner. He was a bronze medalist in the LA Olympics and a veteran of three Olympic teams. We traveled together in Europe for a number of years while I worked for Nike as a meet organizer for its athletes.

For Marni and Corey, the weeks went by too fast. They were out every day, swimming in the warm ocean, climbing rocks as they ventured up the Dunns' River with Brian, the young son of Mark and Annette. Wading from the cool Dunns' River waters into the warm ocean was an exhilarating experience that never got old. It is a must-do activity that most visitors to Jamaica consider a highlight.

We were invited to participate in a meet on one of their grass tracks during our stay. Friendships formed between the athletes, and jersey exchanges became popular. Our distance runners generally bested the Jamaicans, but the host sprinters "cleaned our clocks." Mark continued the summer clinics, which gave many young athletes the opportunity to travel and learn about other cultures. I had been friends with Don Quarrie, one of Jamaica's most famous athletes, for over forty years. DQ, as he was called, attended USC and represented our Strider track club. Having won the 200-meter gold medal at the Montreal Olympics, DQ is one of the most respected individuals in both Jamaica and the track world in general. Since then, Jamaican sprinters, such as Usain Bolt, have dominated international competitions.

27. Pete, Corey, Marni and Joyce at Dunns' River Falls, Jamaica, 1978.

Brazilians with our group: Juaquim Cruz (Olympic gold medalist)
Next to him is Agiberto Guimares, Pete, Coach Luiz Olivares

USA – USSR dual meet in Minsk
from left: Paul Geis – Dick Buekle leading the race

OLYMPIC GAMES

I wish everyone could, at least once, attend the Olympic Games. It is like no other experience. Once every four years, the best athletes in the world come together to test their skills. They are usually joined by countrymen and women dressed in colorful outfits and carrying an impressive array of national flags. I tell my athletes that what they are doing is demonstrating excellence in their event. "Perfection consists not so much in doing extraordinary things, but in doing ordinary things extraordinarily well." I think Bill Toomey taught me that.

Of the four Olympic Games that I was fortunate to witness, the Montreal Games were the sparsest, especially when compared to the grandiose and artistic Munich Olympics of 1972, which spared no expenses. In contrast, Los Angeles suffered from the defections of the Eastern European Communist block countries, which kept the event from being a true and inclusive Olympic Games. However, thanks to the organizational genius of its director, Peter Ueberroth, it became a financial and commercial success that is still unsurpassed. For the first time, an Olympic Games allowed companies to sponsor and arrange advertising for selected events. For example, Fuji paid "big bucks" to be the official film of the Olympics, but then allowed the Kodak Co. to sponsor track and field separately. While Kodak saw significant sales increases because of its sponsorship, Fuji saw minimal returns on its investment and was incredulous (75 percent of Americans polled thought Kodak was the main sponsor). The wealth of corporate sponsorship insured that the Los Angeles Olympics would finish not only in the black, but end up with a huge surplus. Even today, a hefty $120 million surplus remains in the hands of the L.A. Organizing Committee. It is earmarked for youth and sports development in the L.A. area.

Unfortunately, the Atlanta Olympics was somewhat of a sad experience. I felt that it clearly lacked an Olympic spirit and should never have been chosen to host the Games. However, Atlanta marked the beginning of a technological era in which a computer whiz was able to produce spectacular 3D video representations of all the facilities. The IOC officials could visualize what each venue would look like. Atlanta Olympic officials promised impressive sums of cash to make sure the games would run smoothly. Ted Turner loved the deal, since the Olympic stadium would become the post-Olympics home of the Atlanta Braves, all achieved at little expense to his enterprises. Let's face it: Atlanta is mainly a baseball town and not too interested in swimming, wrestling, hammer throwing, and so forth. It suffered from a lack of organization and planning. Tacky vendor stands surrounding the venues made the entrance to the Olympic stadium look more like a swap meet than a gathering of the world's best athletes.

I loved Barcelona and felt that the Spanish games had a special ambience. Many of us can still remember the spectacular opening ceremony when an archer set the Olympic flame ablaze by shooting a lighted arrow all the way up the caldera. The city did not gauge the visitors as walking opportunities to be exploited but instead welcomed them as guests. With the amazing Gaudi-inspired buildings throughout the city, it was an artist's delight.

CHANGES IN TRACK AND FIELD

A fter devoting so many years to the development of track athletes, my involvement in the sport, by necessity, underwent a transition. The glory days of the Southern California Striders ended when shoe companies enticed our best athletes into signing contracts. The club system that was a mainstay in the success of the sport ceased to exist when donors withdrew their financial support. After a tiring day teaching high-school students, I wasn't keen on spending frustrating hours fighting L.A. freeway traffic in order to coach athletes whose motivation was to get paid for running. The professional aspect of track and field wasn't my cup of tea. I still believed in Run for Fun. In 1980, my good friend from my USC days, John Bragg, who was working for Adidas as promotions director and now lived in our area, asked me to arrange track meets in Europe for a couple of the top Adidas athletes. Summer vacation was about to start, and I had no plans, so why not spend a month enjoying all-expenses-paid trips to about eight track meets? It was a wonderful summertime job, allowing me, once again, to be involved in international track and field. I had already met some of the European meet organizers, so I was able to arrange meets for Craig Virgin, the Olympic distance runner from Illinois, James

Robinson, a world-class 800-meter runner, plus two sprinters from Texas. Track is a big sport in Europe, and my athletes got a taste of competing in front of thirty to fifty thousand spectators. We also traveled to Rieti, a small city in Italy known for its Communist-style parades. After my childhood experiences with the Soviets, it was a shock to see the hammer and sickle displayed in red flags. But after a delicious meal in a local restaurant and meeting some of the gracious townspeople, we found that their views were drastically different from the grim sterility of Russian communism. The outgoing Italians loved expressing themselves in a variety of ways, including displaying flags and slogans that advertised the uniqueness of their brand of socialism. Meanwhile, James kept signing autographs for eager youngsters after winning races with his blistering finish. He had never been asked to do that back home, even after winning the NCAA title.

That first year on the European circuit was a valuable learning experience. I had to negotiate with meet organizers such as Enrico Dionisi, who ran the meet in in Viareggio, near Pisa. He was a stereotypical Italian, gesturing with every part of his body to convince me to bring my athletes to Viareggio. He excitedly pleaded with me to bring James Robinson and two sprinters, offering sums of Lira with an astounding number of zeros. I was not yet familiar with the exchange rate for the Lira and accepted his seemingly generous offer. After the meet, the only satisfied person was Enrico, who explained the reason for his country's love of large denomination currency: "Every Italian wants to feel like a millionaire! That's why we like it."

After that first less-than-lucrative experience, I was again approached by Enrico to arrange an 800-meter race between Don Paige, the US 800-meter champion and Olympic champion Sebastian Coe. Seb's father, acting as his son's agent, explained that Seb was fatigued from a tough mile race in Zurich the night before and requested a change of distance. It was a touchy situation, but since both athletes had signed contracts, they agreed to the 800-meter race. I felt badly for the Coes, since we had become friends from previous meets, but Don edged the Olympic champion in an exciting race. This time, I got my zeros figured out, and Enrico was obliged to honor my financial demands, more than making up for previous shortages.

The early meets were often disorganized affairs, with each meet director conducting his meet in his own style. We had to learn the ways each director dealt with athlete managers, payments, travel arrangements, and accommodations. The Scandinavians operated in a totally different fashion from the Italians or French, whose unmatched bureaucracy drove us crazy. The Swiss and Germans prided themselves on punctuality and attention to details, while the Japanese spoiled us with their hospitality. We had to establish close personal and professional relationships with each meet director as well as our own athletes, which often proved to be a challenge.

OUR TRAVELS THRU EUROPE,
by Tom Petranoff, San Diego, California

Pete Petersons was introduced to me by Nike's Tom Sturak and Nelson Farris during the 1980 Olympic Trials. Pete asked me to join his club, The Southern California Striders. We hit it off well from the beginning and shared some great experiences I will cherish forever. Pete played many roles in our relationship, a very influential teacher, my agent, my best friend and father figure all at the same time. He stood up for me and other athletes as a coach and agent. Pete was respected by everyone in track and field, he is a class act. He waited in many long lines to get his athletes paid over the long summers in Europe which we all appreciated, even if it wasn't always spoken.

My favorite story with Pete was when we were on the European tour back in 1982. Back then the athletes, coaches and agents all traveled together on a train or charter plane to the next meet. This *time, we got on the plane, they closed the doors and the plane backed out to the tarmac and stayed there for few minutes. Instead of taking off, they backed back into the gate. The crew called Carl Lewis to the front of the airplane. He had to pay his $1,500 phone bill from our hotel or had to leave the airplane. He paid his bill and we took off to the next destination. Back in the 80's, hotels had mini-bars stocked with liquor in them, but the hotels locked them when we athletes stayed. I got a butter knife when we were at breakfast and started playing with the lock. It took me few minutes but I got it, Open Sesame! We throwers drained many mini bars. One of the runners with us was Tom Byers, he did not drink at all. When we were loading up the bus to leave for the next track meet, the manager of the hotel got on the bus and called Tom Byers to the front. Pete got up to find out what was going on. He was telling the manager that Tom did not drink, even though he looked like he may with his long hippie hair. Pete stood toe to toe with the manager to back Tom. There was a heated exchange but the hotel manager finally relented at the end. As he went to take his seat, Pete looked back at me and gave me a long parental look. I sank in my seat and thought "He knows we throwers did it!" I felt like a kid who was caught with his hand in the candy jar.*

TRAVELS WITH TOM STURAK

My most enjoyable and memorable moments while traveling were shared with my close friend, Tom Sturak. As the director of running promotions for Nike, Tom appointed me as Nike's *Athletics West* running representative. Our main goal was to provide opportunities for international competition for young runners who had graduated from college.

I had known Tom and his wife, Jacqueline, during the 1960s when both were outstanding marathon runners. Jacqueline is still one of the most admired ambassadors for the sport of distance running. As a former winner of the Boston Marathon, she is in demand at distance running events and clinics. Jacqueline also had the courage to challenge the archaic policy of the men's IAA that excluded women from international distance-racing competitions. We all remember the LA Olympics, where Joan Benoit won the first women's marathon race. That was thirty years ago, but before the LA Olympics, the longest race for women was 3,000 meters. Some IOC officials felt that "nobody likes to see women run," and any race longer than 3,000 meters would be boring. However, most track fans vividly remember the infamous tripping incident between Zola Budd and Mary Slaney in the Los

Angeles games. Thanks to Jacqueline and the women's groups who gathered at the first World Track Championships in Helsinki in 1983, the 5,000-meter, 10,000-meter, and marathon races might have never been part of the Olympics. Joan Benoit's stunning win in the marathon in 1984 was the crowning achievement in the fight to give women equal opportunity in Olympic sports. Jacqueline's perseverance extended beyond the Olympics, resulting in women being allowed to run 5,000- and 10,000-meter races in all international competitions.

28. Pete and Tom Sturak in Finland, 1985.

Tom's love for running was matched by his passion for literature, contemporary music, art, vintage red wine, and the beauty of the English language. He was a voracious reader of nearly everything he could get his hands on. One of his bags contained nothing but books and periodicals. He also took pride in his background as a

Slovak from Eastern Europe, reminding friends that he and his cousin, Andy Warhol, attended the same classes in their Pennsylvania high school. Some people thought of Tom as a cantankerous intellectual who had little patience with people who were less than candid. But eventually they learned to appreciate his keen sense of humor and the refreshing ways that he demonstrated his enjoyment of life.

We became traveling junkies, traversing numerous time zones during summer cross-continent jaunts. We witnessed many records and shared "the good, the bad, and the ugly" parts of international track competition for fifteen years. Luckily, we had so many things in common that even the bad and ugly parts took on their own excitement. Pat Devaney's description of the European tour said it best: "It was something like a circus of traveling track gypsies, with coaches, trainers, athletes, shoe representatives, managers, and meet organizers all filling the three rings." Tom and I were able to forge personal and professional relationships with world-class athletes and meet organizers. The organizers were an interesting lot. Each had his own unique background that shaped his view of the sport. Among the more memorable personalities that we encountered were a doctor-on-leave in Sweden, a stamp collector from Norway, a renowned architect from Berlin, and a former policeman in England. The Swiss were known for the insurance company executives that became meet organizers. With so many different backgrounds and personalities, it was a challenge to establish a lasting working relationship with each director. We found that the approach we needed to take varied considerably. It could be safely assumed that most were knowledgeable about our sport and had a good understanding of the financial climate in their country. Most individuals were prominent enough in their country to secure the financial backing needed to organize a competition. They knew which banks to approach. They preferred managers who were genuinely and deeply attached to the sport, a description that fortunately applied to Tom and me. But over time, professional agents became more and more aggressive in their negotiations with meet organizers. They did not hesitate to use cutthroat tactics to secure the appearance fees that they thought to be appropriate. They often persuaded athletes to switch managers, which practically eliminated representatives like us.

Tom's place in Nike history goes back to the days when Nike was a struggling shoe company with typical entrepreneurial growing pains. The earliest representatives sold shoes out of their cars while simultaneously trying to establish an identity in the track community. Tom was hired as their running promotions director, and along with his friend, Jon Gregorio, came up with the idea of using famous runners for promotion. They had become friends with the best British distance runners, Sebastian Coe (currently the president of the IAAF), Steve Ovett, Steve Cram, and Kenyan Henry Rono. The decision was made to offer contracts in which each athlete would wear Nike gear and promote Nike products. Agreements were finalized in taverns between drinks of beer, using napkins to affix the necessary signatures. They became the first European or African runners to wear the Nike logo. Nike had not established a specific direction until Phil Knight, Jeff Johnson, and Coach Bill Bowerman took the reins of the operation. They encouraged their employees to be daring, and the company soon became known for its willingness to try some of the wild plans that were eventually proposed. Nike had offices scattered throughout Beaverton, but they had already purchased land for a spacious complex. They tapped into the available pool of talented young innovators and came up with revolutionary colors and designs. Jeff Johnson, one of Bowerman's former runners, designed the "swoosh" logo and the name Nike, the Greek Goddess of victory. Most of us have heard of Bill's kitchen experiment in which a waffle iron inspired the design of a running shoe. Bowerman's waffle iron was destroyed, but the Waffle Trainer became one of the most popular shoes of its time. Nike's ability to set new design and technical standards, along with its carefully crafted advertising campaigns, laid the groundwork for a future billion-dollar mega-corporation. By sponsoring international athletic teams such as Manchester United, Arsenal, and Barcelona, and athletes such as Kobe Bryant, Michael Johnson, and Michael Jordan, Nike has secured its place as a world leader in the sale of athletic equipment and apparel. It is no longer the intimate operation that Tom and I experienced during the company's infancy.

29. Pete congratulating James Robinson after an 800m win in Oslo, Norway, 1982.

As other shoe innovations began attracting customers, Nike's swoosh logo helped make the company famous and profitable. Bill Bowerman and ten other investors raised enough money to set up Nike as a publically owned company. The original department heads were given the choice of a lifetime contract or stock options. Those who took the stocks became instant millionaires, while others remained with the company for decades. Unfortunately, Tom was let go when he refused to fire a fellow employee whose incompetency had caused major problems within the organization. Even though the employee deserved to be fired, Tom simply didn't have the stomach to assume the role of corporate assassin. He realized that he was not cut out to be a businessman. Having earned a doctorate in English at UCLA, he still had interests in other pursuits. Tom, however, loved track and wanted to continue with the sport at some level. Fortunately, his friend, Pat Devaney, hired him to represent Reebok athletes in Europe. I still had my Nike position, so we were reunited and, once again, were able to travel with our athletes. Although we worked for different employers, we still shared hotel rooms and went through the many and varied gyrations necessary to receive an athlete's pay from meet organizers. We pleaded with meet organizers, shared *The International Herald Tribune* whenever we could find it, and watched many world records be broken. In order to escape the hectic atmosphere of big-time track meets, we went for runs whenever we could get away. We were called the "old couple," since we were the oldest managers on the tour. Being with such an enlightening individual as Tom was rewarding and fun. We loved browsing through bookstores, always on the lookout for rare books and manuscripts. He was excited when he ran across the manuscript of *They Shoot Horses, Don't They?* in a Berlin book store. Even though it was in German, he felt he had found something special. He had written his dissertation for his UCLA doctorate on the life and work of the novelist, Horace

McCoy. His material had provided the background for the movie, which won the best actress award for Jane Fonda. Tom also served as an adviser to Sidney Pollack, who directed the film. On our travels, Tom always carried an extra pen and pencil and an extra pair of glasses, all of which he was always losing. Being an English major and former professor, he hated seeing misspelled words and incorrect grammar, especially in newsprint. He would have a fit today, seeing the Fox Network listing new words such as "selfie" (misspelled as "slefie") in Webster's dictionary. Tom always took out his pen and underlined grammar mistakes and misspelled words. He considered the European *Herald Tribune* to be the best newspaper, since he seldom found a mistake. Jacqueline commented, "He had a rare sense of humor that could rival any late-night talk show host." As a manager, his athletes and meet organizers admired him. He struck up a friendship with Henry Rono, the fast-emerging running sensation from Kenya. Tom was concerned about Henry's drinking and his habit of squandering his winnings in Europe. He was hoping that the organizers would treat him fairly. One morning after a meet, Tom found Henry asleep, with different currencies spread all over the desk, along with a variety of airline tickets. Henry loved getting airline tickets, even though transportation was already provided for him. As far as currencies, he assured Tom that he had deposited them in various banks throughout Europe. When asked which banks and their locations, Henry replied that he wasn't sure, but hoped to locate them someday.

30. Pete with Louise Ritter - Gold medalist - Seoul Olympics, 1988.

Our travel to Belfast during the upheaval, or civil war between the Catholics and Protestants, was an unnerving experience. We were escorted through groups of angry demonstrators by heavily armed British soldiers. These incidents made us realize how tense the civil unrest had become. Before entering our hotel, we had to go through a series of checkpoints, each surrounded by barbed wire. Since the meet was planned in the spirit of friendship and was an attempt to bring the two sides together, it went as well as could be expected.

Continuing to Italy, Tom had a very unusual experience with Sandro Giovanelli, the organizer of the Sestriere meet. Being a meet organizer in Italy can be a nerve-racking experience, even for a seasoned veteran like Sandro. The usual glitches become routine: people assigned to pick up athletes or meet officials fail to show up, which is compounded by hotel telephone systems creating nightmarish communication problems. Despite the challenges, everything miraculously falls into place at the last minute, and athletes and coaches leave Italy in good spirits. After the Sestriere meet, Tom found Sandro in a dark hall where he was paying the athletes' managers the appearance money that had been agreed upon before the meet. Sandro was exhausted from all the pre-meet complications, but he asked Tom which athletes he had competing in the meet. Tom told him that his 5,000-meter runner was promised $500. Being so tired, Sandro proceeded to dish out $5,000! "No! No!" Tom explained as he returned the overpayment. Sandro has a reputation throughout Europe as a tireless director, but he showed us that even the best are human.

Bert Bonano, who had put on our national championships in San Jose in June, invited an East German track official to his meet. The East German was the organizer of a major meet in East Berlin. He wanted to talk to US managers about bringing some of our athletes to his meet in July. The meet hotel, The Sheraton, was hosting a large space-themed masquerade convention during the same weekend as the meet. The entire hotel was overrun with "spaced out" enthusiasts, most dressed in bizarre costumes. Our East German visitor was shocked. He kept shaking his head, asking if this was how Americans normally behaved. This was his first impression of life in the United States, an impression that we were sure would provide him with entertaining stories to share when he returned to Europe.

Despite his bizarre introduction to American culture, he invited us to bring some of our athletes to Berlin while the Wall was still intact. Some of the managers accepted his offer and agreed to bring a few athletes who were brave enough to venture behind the iconic barrier between West and East. It would be our first opportunity to view a Communist country and see the Wall from our plane. Approaching Tegel airport, we crossed over the depressing maze of reinforced wire-mesh fences and the barren section of empty space that separated the two cities.

After landing at Tegel, we faced the formidable task of clearing passport control and customs. Tony Campbell, our outspoken and happy-go-lucky manager, was quickly reminded by the East German officials to tone down our loud discussions. The dour-faced officials made it clear that they weren't in the mood for jokes or snide comments as we waited to present our documents, so we accommodated our hosts with uncharacteristic (for us) dead silence as we waited for what seemed to be an eternity. We were first in line, and the officials wanted to intimidate us. Finally, an officer appeared from an adjoining room, and with a dramatic pirouette of his bureaucratic tool, stamped Tony's passport. We all exhaled a sigh of relief.

We had to exchange some dollars for the worthless East German currency. We found out that the only items we could buy in the lobby were combs, toothbrushes, paper, and trinkets. After settling down in our hotel, I received a frantic phone call from my lady sprinter who was shrieking that her bathtub water was light brown and foul smelling. What could I do, except say, "Welcome to East Germany"? Their beer had little resemblance to ours, tasting flat with a noticeable gasoline smell. We had an opportunity to see the famous East German women sprinters, who were rumored to have received the help of some powerful vitamins and other unusual additives. Our suspicions were confirmed when we saw them cruise the 400-meter run in forty-eight seconds.

After the meet, when all managers had finally assembled for payment, we became concerned that we might have problems securing dollars or any other type of Western currency. The longer we waited, usually well into the early morning, the more concerned we had become. What if they were unable to honor our agreements? When it was time for us to adjourn for breakfast, most of us had been paid, albeit in a variety of currencies. Some athletes tried to change the useless East German marks back to dollars, but that was strictly "verboten."

When I agreed to accompany Tom on the European jaunts, I didn't realize that it would involve nearly twenty track meets spread over a three-month season. A track meet every three days involved constant packing and unpacking and minimal sleep. Looking back, I must have underestimated what a challenging and tiring undertaking it would involve. Having Tom around as a sounding board for the inevitable frustrations made it bearable. Teachers don't get paid for the three summer months, so I was hoping to supplement my income. Luckily I was able to take Joyce with me to some of the meets. While waiting for the Berlin meet to start, Joyce and Coach Pat Connolly crossed the East German border at Check Point Charlie and immediately saw how drab and colorless East Germany had become. On the same trip, she was able to return to West Berlin and watch the ISTAF Grand Prix Meet. She experienced shivers as she and sixty thousand fellow spectators watched athletes of every race and nationality compete in the same stadium where Hitler witnessed the 1936 Olympics.

On another trip in 1982, Joyce loved roaming through the streets of Monte Carlo and luxuriating in the Lowe's Hotel, situated next to a famous Monte Carlo casino. With one of the most prestigious meets in Europe, the Weltklasse, on our schedule, it was easy to visit our Swiss friends in Biel. Having Marni with me at the Paris Grand Prix meet was very special because I was able to share the excitement of an international meet with her. In 1985, we were pleased to have her with us when we went to Hengelo, Netherlands, for a small-town meet. In Amsterdam, I put her on a train to Bonn to visit friends of our family, letting her gain confidence as a lone traveler in Europe.

As Corey matured, it became her turn to experience the unique flavor of hurried travel in Europe. Being anything but a shy girl, she decided to venture down to the beautiful beach at Monaco for a few hours and go skinny-dipping with the natives. Olivier, the son of Jackie Delapierre, escorted her to the Swiss Alps on another trip. These European experiences enabled Marni and Corey to become comfortable traveling alone. Corey eventually spent six weeks doing research in the mountain regions of Nepal and three years working in an ashram in India. Having my girls with me made my job easier. They also saw how intense my job was with often-unhappy athletes demanding more money, or voicing complaints about inclement weather conditions or taxes taken out of their income, etc. They soon learned about the downside of my assignment: long waits in hotel hallways after each meet to collect athletes' prize money, arranging travel to the next city, and attending to injured athletes. The French were notorious for their bureaucratic tradition of requiring countless detailed forms that needed to be signed in triplicate. They never seemed to trust us, and often claimed that such-and-such an athlete never competed in their meet. Of course, requiring us to provide more documents, including proof that an athlete was in fact in Paris.

The most memorable aspect of our summer travels was being able to know and represent so many Olympians and world-record holders. They have always showed appreciation for the service we tried to provide and have remained valued friends. Doug Padilla and Henry Marsh from BYU were part of my outstanding distance group. Others in our traveling entourage were Mark Crear, double medalist in the hurdles, Hollis Conway, the happy-go-lucky high jumper from Louisiana, Annette Peters, Olympian Louise Ritter, Tom Byers, Chuck Aragon, steeplechaser Brian Diemer, the bronze medalist in the LA Olympics, world-record-holding triple jumper, Willie Banks, and Olympians Kenny Harrison and Al Joyner. Also joining us were Tim and Julie Bright, "Big Ben" Plucknett, who set a new world record in the discus, Randy Barnes, Olympic champion in the shot put, and James Robinson, not only a huge success as a 800-meter runner, but also as a very supportive and helpful traveler.

WAITING IN LINES TO GET ATHLETES FEES

During the early 1980's we managers had to endure a taxing, frustrating and tiring ritual of collecting athlete's appearance fee and travel expenses. These usually took place long after midnight, after the organizers and sponsors had finished their after-meet dinners. We could find payments made under the stadium bleachers or in hotel hallways. These *'under-the-grandstand-payment-lines'* only required a signature, although hardly ever did anyone ever sign their name, often faking Carl Lewis or Jim Ryun's signature. Some organizers often did not tell us where we could pick up the agreed-upon money. It became a game of guessing. But as the meets became more popular with more spectators, the organizers wanted to make the after-meet payments easier for them and us. It was a ritual that taxed our energies and robbed us of our sleep. Tom and I spent countless hours in the hallways when we could have relaxed over a beer in a lounge. I pitied the poor hotel guests who saw long lines of managers in front of their doors, practically blocking their entrance.

Our first order of business was finding out on what floor and in which room the exhausted organizers (not to mention their sour mood) were carrying out the payments. Payment locations included an old tower away from the track in Aarhus, Denmark, a dark basement in Sestriere, a building next to the stadium in Ingolstadt, Germany, a restaurant in Rhede, Germany, and even on an US battleship that was moored in Naples harbor (where we ate meals) for the meet in Formia, Italy. Once we were instructed to wait for a Volkswagen bus that would arrive at noon in an Italian meet. It arrived hours later and we almost missed our trip to the next meet. Andy Norman was the most practical organizer whose treasurer often paid in hotel lobbies, or even on planes going to the next meet. Berlin was frustrating some years when Rudi Thiel chose a leisure boat on a lake in Berlin, often waiting way past midnight, or even at the next track meet.

31. Petersons family in Carmel, California, 1984.

A CAST OF UNFORGETTABLE
CHARACTERS

No description of my eighteen years of travel through Europe would be complete without giving credit to the talented and personable athletes who made my journeys so rewarding.

WILLIE BANKS

One of my most enjoyable associations was with Willie Banks. His name became synonymous with triple jumping. With the ever-present Walkman attached to his lithe body, I can't recall any other athlete who has contributed as much to his event as Willie. His contagious smile and spontaneous enthusiasm made him one of the most popular athletes in Europe. I call him a troubadour of our sport. Initially, I arranged an indoor competition in Tokyo, where the large crowd instantly adopted him as a favorite. After that, everyone on the international circuit looked forward to seeing him flashing his grin while sailing along the runway. He made his event more than just a hop, skip, and a jump. Spectators quickly picked him out from the other competitors as he listened to his Walkman while executing warm-up jumps. When some Nordic meet organizers were hesitant to feature the triple jump because fans considered it to be boring, Willie took matters into his own hands. A Stockholm meet organizer told him that they were thinking about eliminating the triple jump because Swedish fans favored the javelin and discus. Upon hearing this, Willie decided that he had heard enough negative talk about his beloved event. You could notice that Willie was becoming animated because he promised the organizer that he and his fellow jumpers "would shake up the joint" and put on a show. With entertainer Willie and his two other American jumpers taking turns, they began rhythmic clapping. A few fans joined in, and soon everyone in the stadium was clapping in unison. Willie's theatrics drew the attention of the entire stadium, and the meet organizers took note that the triple jump had suddenly become one of the most popular events on the program.

We made an agreement to compete in Turku, which had hosted elite competitions for decades. The meet organizer, Pekka Paakanen, added an extra incentive for fans, indicating they could win a prize if they correctly picked Willie's winning mark. All action came to a stop when Willie made his jumps. Afterward, youngsters ran after him, seeking his autograph, so I urged him to follow me to a safer place on the first row of the second tier bleachers. Big mistake. They almost pushed us over the railing. From then on the triple jump was included in meets throughout Europe. Thanks to Willie, a track-and-field tradition had been born. In today's meets, spectators routinely clap their hands in unison when a jumper is at the head of the runway. Although he lit up stadiums wherever we went, I was always impressed with Willie's ability to show his appreciation and gratitude. He made a point of sending thank-you cards and letters to each of the meet organizers for inviting him to their meets. To this day, he remains one of the most influential athletes in our sport: a true ambassador of goodwill wherever he goes.

Willie was one of the few track stars who insisted on having his mother accompany him on many of his trips. He wanted to make sure his mother had a chance to experience the excitement of an international meet in Europe. Some meet directors were aware of the petty grumbling about Willie's insistence on having his mother join him, but Andy Norman responded curtly, "One must always respect his mother!" Having seen Willie and his American teammates perform on Euro Sport TV, Europeans developed a love affair with our athletes, especially the sprinters and jumpers. They were fascinated and surprised when big Ben Plucknett had the audacity to step into the discus the ring while a 400-meter race was being contested. The fans, however, were rewarded when they saw his discus take wing, resulting in a new world record of 235 feet, a performance they will never forget. With their tradition of producing great throwers, the Swedes adored the event and forgave Ben for his perceived indiscretion. The Swedes still reminisce about Ben's audacious performance that evening, producing a mark that stood as a record for five years. In a Zurich meet, we saw Randy Barnes, the Olympic shotput champion, step into the ring for his latest duel with the Swiss favorite, Werner Guenthor. The next day's headlines featured a picture of the two big competitors shaking hands. Randy had won in Zurich, but Werner beat him in the next competition.

32. Willie Banks, the troubadour of track and field
on the victory stand in Japan, 1988.

RANDY BARNES

The muscular world-record holder in the shot put loved sleep more than even food. I was always worried that he would over-sleep and miss the bus to the next meet. No worries—he always made it. On our trip to a meet in a small town outside Tokyo, his luggage never made it in time for the competition. Despite my warnings to always carry the essentials you will need for the com-petition, he put his throwing gear and special shoes in his main luggage. We scurried to locate another pair of shoes, but in Japan it was next to impossible to find shoes that would fit a six-foot-five, three-hundred-pound behemoth. Randy resigned himself to doing without his favorite shoes and put his innovative talents on display by designing a special tape wrap for his street shoes. The photographers had a field day taking pictures of the celebrity shot putter in the process of carefully taping his shoes. The photos were plastered into major newspapers throughout Japan. Despite slipping and sliding in the shot put circle, he still managed to win. I have never seen so many typically reserved Japanese laughing hysterically about the unfortunate but unforeseen event. Evidently, it was tremendous entertainment, because they invited us back for next year's meet, provided that Randy would bring proper shoes.

ROCHELLE STEVENS was one of my favorite athletes, because she always looked after me. She was a gold medalist in the 4x400-meter in the 1996 Atlanta Olympics, a silver medalist in the 4x400-meter at Barcelona, as well as the 400-meter champion at the World Championships in Gothenburg, Sweden. I was fortunate to have such an elegant athlete in my group as we traveled throughout Europe. Being a highly organized but compassionate person, she realized that at times I was the person in need of being looked after. "Pete, did she end up in lane eight?" (The worst lane for a 400-meter runner.) I thought she would fire me, but instead, she kept me on and we had a ball traveling to big meets and smaller meets, like Rhede in Germany. Today we exchange Christmas greetings every year, and I always ask her: "Rochelle, I can line you up for a meet in Europe, and you can have lane eight. Are you interested?" Today Rochelle is a very successful businesswoman, the founder and CEO of a health and wellness spa. She even ran for a public office. Rochelle loves giving back to her sport by promoting physical and mental fitness. Her Foundation assists ten thousand track-and-field participants in Collierville, Tennessee.

TOM PETRANOFF'S javelin left his hand at a perfect thirty-degree angle and kept on sailing, higher and farther, gliding against the wind, until it hit the ground at 327 feet, 2 inches (99.72 meters);

a new world record. The spectators at the Pepsi Invitational meet at UCLA in April 1983 were shocked to see the javelin travel farther than the length of a football field. The Striders athlete turned the athletics world upside down. Working with Nike's Athletics West traveling team, I became Tom's manager and he converted to an Athletics West athlete. We traveled to Scandinavia to challenge the best Finnish and German throwers. It was fun to see Tom blossom into an international star overnight. He exploded on the scene with his enthusiasm and energy. Tom loved talking to the reporters, fans, or anyone else who was interested. He was always willing to sign autographs and pose for pictures. I enjoyed his visits when we were able to discuss his performance and plans for the next meet. He always brought a bag full of every kind of vitamin, mineral, and protein pill, educating me about the essentials of proper nutrition and urging me to "clean up my act." We went from the famous Helsinki meet (best place to throw javelin) where eager Finns were able to see him for the first time, to many smaller meets in Sweden, Norway, and other countries in Europe.

The spectators were excited to see the javelins float like Frisbees thrown against the wind. The javelin became one of the featured events. Whenever we went for walks through towns, people would recognize him and were thrilled when Tom would autograph their shirts, hats, etc. Unfortunately, after being favored to win, he had a disappointing performance at the Los Angeles Olympics. After Los Angeles, Tom moved to South Africa, with hopes of representing that country in the Olympics. While in South Africa, he set many records and designed a children's javelin that was as aeronautically precise as a standard competition javelin, but was competitively priced and safe for children. He eventually became disappointed with life in South Africa and returned to the United States, where he is now busy coaching his daughter Leah in the javelin (what else?), hoping that she might become the family's next Olympian. He has never stopped innovating, creating special exercises for the javelin. And he is now promoting his latest "Turbo Jav" for schools.

World Record, 327.2, 1983

33. Tom Petranoff, world record holder in javelin, UCLA, 1983.

RUNNING THE SHOW: MEET DIRECTORS ON THE EUROPEAN CIRCUIT

During the years that Tom and I were involved in ferrying athletes through Europe, we had the privilege of working with many talented and dedicated meet organizers. They spoke a variety of languages but shared a passion for our sport. They were an interesting lot, with each organizer bringing a unique background to the table.

Even though much of our dealings revolved around organizational and financial details, I have always tried to engage the organizers as special people in my life. They were appreciative if you could put aside business for a while and get to know them as individuals, which turned out to be the most enjoyable part of our relationships. Tom and I felt that we were not treated as typical business-only agents, but that we were respected for the enthusiasm and honesty that came from our decades of involvement at all levels of the sport. Like Willie Banks, Tom and I always followed a stay with a post card or letter thanking the directors for being such gracious hosts. When they saw that I loved their meet enough to bring my family, we were able to establish close relationships that have lasted for years.

Tom Byers leading Sebastian Coe in Zurich

Associated Press

— Oh boy. Sinä teit sen, diivaeleinen brittien Steve Ovett jäi 52 sadasosasekunnilla . . . USA:n Tom Byersin valmentaja ei tiedä kuinka lämpimästi onnittelisi valmennettavaansa.

Long way from home

Lake Lindero resident and Agoura High School social studies teacher Atis Petersons, right, congratulates Tom Byers after the American upset Britain's Steve Ovett in a 1,500-meter race in Oslo, Norway, Friday. Petersons helps coach some of America's top distance runners in his spare time. (AP photo)

Byers the best in Oslo

SVEIN-ARNE HANSEN, NORWAY

On our first trips to Europe, I found that some meet organizers were reluctant to accept my athletes. Most of my runners were young and had never competed outside the United States. Even my close friend, Svein-Arne of the prestigious Bislett Games in Oslo, hesitated to invite Tom Byers, who had recently won a big mile race in Eugene. Tom was the type of runner who loved running from the front. I told Svein-Arne that Tom's front-running style would guarantee a fast pace, but I pleaded with him to not include Tom as a designated "rabbit."

Despite my request, the word got out that Tom would be willing to push the tempo as a rabbit and drop out after three laps. In one unforgettable race as a designated rabbit, Tom ran his usual fast first and second laps, but this time, after three laps, he had a 50-meter lead on the field. To everyone's surprise, including mine, he decided to keep running. The world's top milers were furious when Tom held his lead and won the race. The sophisticated Bislett crowd had previously witnessed many memorable races, but was totally stunned that a "rabbit" had outsmarted everyone: spectators, racers, and meet directors. Oslo track fans who had witnessed the race still consider it to be a classic David versus Goliath drama played out on a running track. Last year, twenty years after the famous race, Svein-Arne invited Tom and his wife Ann to be special guests at their annual banquet.

Svein-Arne and I became a good friends, and he made sure my athletes would always be welcome in his meet. He is well known in Norway as one of the world's most accomplished stamp collectors. His involvement in Norwegian athletics was a hobby, but he was rewarded by the lasting relationships he was able to build with coaches, athletes, and track officials. One year he chose a rookie runner to set the pace for the 800-meter race. Unfortunately, this rabbit did such a poor job that even the fans hissed. After the race, Svein confronted him and asked him a simple question: do you have a camera? The runner nodded his head and showed it to him. Svein told him to be sure to take lots of pictures, since he would never be invited to Oslo again. I treasure the trips I have taken with Svein. On one stopover in Copenhagen, he had to go to a restroom, so he asked me to guard his briefcase. He whispered that the case contained over a million dollars' worth of stamps that he was taking to a dealer's convention. I had never been so nervous and could not help maintaining a death grip on the briefcase for the entire time he was in the bathroom.

Each European meet created its own aura, with Oslo showcasing distance runners, Zurich a premier venue for sprinters and jumpers, and Lausanne being famous for sold-out extravaganzas featuring sprinters such as Usain Bolt. Monaco became known as a pole-vaulter's meet, Berlin concentrated on featuring their own outstanding weight-event athletes, and Rieti attracted more than its share of world-record-setting middle-distance runners. Brussels was traditionally the last meet of the summer and usually chose the events that had produced the best results and fittest athletes from previous meets.

34. Mary Decker Slaney and Svein-Arnie Hansen

ANDREAS BRUEGGER, SWITZERLAND

One of the earliest and most satisfying experiences for me was creating a friendship with Andreas Bruegger, who established Zurich's *Weltklasse* meet in 1973. It eventually became one of the premiere meetings in Europe, today welcoming an impressive $4 million of support from Swiss banks. After Armin Harry first broke the 100-meter record, the meet has since produced more world records than any other on the circuit. It developed into more than just a track meeting, becoming famous as one of the prominent cultural and social events in Europe. Every athlete dreams of being invited to the Zurich meet. Joyce and I have traveled to Switzerland for nearly twenty summers and have developed a valued friendship with Andreas and his wife Doris. Our family has fond memories of our visits in their beautiful chalet in Grindelwald. He respected Tom and I because we truly loved the sport, and considered the Zurich meeting as an enjoyable social event rather than just a "business as usual" arrangement.

35. Corey, Joyce and Marni with good friends Doris and Andreas Bruegger near Grindelwald, Switzerland, 1979

JACKIE DELAPIERRE, SWITZERLAND

Most of the organizers have successful careers separate from the part of their lives devoted to track and field. This also applies to Jackie Delapierre from Lausanne, and his son, Olivier. Besides his business interests, Jackie has held high positions with both the IOC and the IAAF. Just recently, Olivier was appointed as the go-between the IOC and future Olympic Games organizers.

The early meets were held next to Lake Geneva on a small track facility. Those who competed in those early years remember the beauty of the setting, with spectators crowded right next to the track. The runners, no doubt, also remember the swarms of tiny mosquitoes that covered their faces or had to be swallowed as they were performing.

Upon Olivier's graduation from high school, Jackie wanted him to come to California for a year and attend a college. Joyce came to the rescue and succeeded in getting Olivier enrolled in the scenic Santa Barbara Community College. He told us that college was easy for him, compared with the strict Swiss standards. He almost passed the driver's test on his first try and got his social security card. A few years later, he received a summons for jury duty. I explained that he was a Swiss citizen and the only way he would consider coming was if they paid his way. We didn't hear from them again!

Years later, Jackie was kind enough to fly Joyce and me to Olivier's and Laurence's wedding in Switzerland and France. The Swiss have some of Europe's strictest rules for driving under the influence of alcohol, so after the memorable Swiss wedding, Jackie arranged to have the dinner celebration in a castle in France, high above the city of Les Bains. Guests were free to enjoy their wine throughout the night, capping off the celebration with a huge bonfire and strong coffee in the early morning hours.

After all these years, we feel very close to the Delapierre family. Olivier and Laurence now have two children, we are proud to call their family our friends.

WILFRIED MEERT, BELGIUM

Wilfried and his wife Annie became one of the driving forces in the creation of the *Ivo Van Damme* meeting in Brussels, Belgium. I first met the talented Ivo Van Damme at the Swiss training center in Biel, Switzerland in 1976, where our Saudi athletes were training for the Montreal Olympics. There was something different about Van Damme. The tall, bearded, powerfully-built runner struck an imposing picture of a character that could have easily come out of a Rembrandt painting. He was an impressive young man who befriended people with his personality. My runners were shocked how easily he ran the 400m intervals. How fortunate that I was in Montreal to see him win silver medals in both the 800m and the 1500m in the Olympics. It was both inspirational and memorable. The track world was shocked when he died in a head-on car accident in France, just a year later. The whole nation mourned his death. A similar accident just a year earlier had taken Steve Prefontaine's life. It was only fitting to name the meet after him. Today Brussels is one of the premiere meets, thanks to Wilfried's efforts, a part of the Diamond League, attracting 40,000 spectators. Most of the spectators who stay after the meet are treated to a free outdoor concert in the same stadium.

Wilfried Meert has been gracious throughout the years, giving many of my athletes the opportunity to partake. Even after I had retired, he invited me to be his guest in Brussels. It was relaxing not to worry about athletes, sitting one row below King Baudouin. Wilfried and his wife, Annie are well-known wine connoisseurs. Tom Sturak, who is also quite knowledgeable about wine, was invited to dinner with Wilfried and Annie in Prague. They discussed Tom's athletes, with Wilfried agreeing to include his sprinter and steeplechaser for the meet. However, some months later, when the Brussels meet approached, Wilfried said "no" to Tom's athletes. Tom reminded him about the fine 1965 Rothschild wine they were sharing when the agreement was made and Wilfried quickly reconsidered, saying, "If you are unable to remember runners' names, it helps to remember the wine you were drinking."

SANDRO GIOVANELLI, ITALY

Sandro Giovanelli was "Mr. Athletico" in Italy, who managed both the Rome Grand Prix meet in the ancient Olympic stadium and a handful of smaller meets. His most challenging project involved building a track at a ski resort in the Italian Alps, at an altitude of over seven thousand feet. The Sestriere meeting was designed to give sprinters and jumpers an advantage in setting new records. I loved the secluded location, with the snow-covered mountains surrounding the track providing welcome relief from the oppressive heat of the Italian summer. The one problem, however, was dealing with the unpredictable weather, which could include snowfall. Since the inclement weather usually arrived after lunch, the meet started around ten in the morning. During most of the years that I attended, the sun kept the clouds away until the afternoon, and we could sleep in. However, if the weather report predicted foul weather, we needed to be prepared to start at 9:00 a.m. The results during the years that my athletes and I attended were impressive, with new world records in the long jump and many national records in the sprints and hurdles. Sandro was able to award Fiat and Alfa Romeo cars for the best performers and a Ferrari for the world-record jumper. Usually, there was no problem in getting athletes to Sestriere. I was able to make arrangements for Corey to join me. We had a spectacular train ride from our friend's home in Switzerland, over the Alpine passes and descending into Milan, from which we survived a cramped car ride all the way up to Sestriere. Corey is an outdoors person, so she loved the refreshing mountain air and the scenic hiking trails.

JEAN-PIERRE SCHOEBEL, MONACO

The Hercules Diamond Meet in the principality of Monaco was an event not to be missed. It is one of the highlights of every athlete's track experience. Where else would we be able to meet Prince Albert, described by many as a "track nut," in person at the beautiful stadium, or at the banquet following the competition? All of us were looking forward to competing in the French Riviera, a beautiful setting with guaranteed balmy weather. A feeling of calm and relaxation fell over our group as we approached the Nice airport. Any tension we carried with us disappeared upon viewing the turquoise blue water and elegant white hotels of the Riviera below us. Everyone was in a good mood and eager to unpack bags and get into swimsuits. Jean-Pierre Schoebel, the meet organizer, spared no expense in making sure everyone in our group was well taken care of. The spacious Hyatt Hotel, overlooking Monte Carlo Casino, was probably the best hotel we stayed in on our tour. The Nikaia meet held in Nice was unfortunately discontinued, so Monaco took over, and since its beginning, has challenged Zurich as the most successful in achieving outstanding results. No one worried about rain, and with weather similar to Southern California, it stayed warm late into the evening. Some athletes, after accumulating earnings from previous meets, couldn't resist the temptation to increase their earnings at the casino, which was conveniently located in our hotel. Most of the athletes soon found out that it was tougher beating the system at the tables than winning a cash payout for their performance on the track. Prince Albert, who loves all sports, was responsible for helping Jean-Pierre fulfill his pledge that athletes and coaches would be treated to a first-class experience in Monaco. The prince loved to meet and talk with all of us. His memory was remarkable; people who had met him years earlier were surprised when Albert remembered their names. After a fabulous dinner with spectacular entertainment, Albert presented awards to the best performers. Jean-Pierre and I became friends from the start. He was a physical fitness teacher, so we compared the responsibilities of our jobs and found that we had a lot in common. His oldest son, Robin, who was six foot six and an outstanding volleyball player in France, had just graduated from high school. He was interested in competing in the United States, so I volunteered to help him find a US school that might meet his needs as a student-athlete. Jean-Pierre had produced a video of his son in action on the volleyball court, which I forwarded to the Pepperdine, Cal State Northridge, and USC coaches. All were impressed, but since the NCAA rules do not allow scholarships to be granted to athletes who have received prior financial help, he was out of luck. Even though Robin had only received food money and travel expenses from his club, they still considered him to be a professional. Robin ended up playing for a small university in Canada and enjoyed the experience. Our families have kept in touch and exchanged holiday greetings. Jean-Pierre kept reminding us that we were always welcome as his guests. In 1976, after a challenging year in Saudi Arabia, Joyce, Marni and Corey were able to join me for the Hercules meet, where we were especially appreciative of the first-class accommodations and access to cultural attractions. Marni and I visited Monaco another time, when our friends took us on a leisure trip after the Nice meet.

ANDY NORMAN, GREAT BRITAIN

Perhaps the best help we received in getting young athletes introduced to European meets came from Andy Norman, the ex-cop from London. Nobody worked harder to arrange entry into meets with only a few days' notice. His influence was instrumental in introducing athletes to competition in England, Belfast,

Budapest, Norway, and Germany. He and his friend, Svein-Arne Hansen, the Oslo meet organizer, worked together as a team. They were always looking for young, talented American athletes, so he made sure that we were able to travel from one meet to another without being stranded. Even though he was a typical Englishman who never missed an opportunity to proclaim the superiority of the British system, we still loved him. He was a former cop whose job was to interrogate criminal suspects, so he was skilled in determining whether or not a person was telling the truth. Athletes who were less than honest about their accomplishments were never invited back to his meets, so everyone quickly learned it was best to be straight with him. Whenever he approached me about the next meet, I knew that he would want me to give him a list of my athletes. After a careful look, Andy made check marks after each name, looked me in the eye, and proclaimed, using the typical British pejorative, "Rubbish! Rubbish! Rubbish!" My heart sank after each mark, but then, with a sly smile on his face, he asked me, "How much do you want for the whole lot?" In many ways, he ran a very unconventional operation. Often he would organize meets on a few days' notice. His finance man always accompanied him, often paying money in hotel lobbies or on planes in public view. As a member of IAAF council, Andy was able to arrange meets in Budapest to be televised on British TV. From the television income, he could pay the fees of both Hungarian and Western athletes. Andy made sure all of my athletes were part of the arrangement, even though it involved a lot of drama and improvisation.

One of the most unusual meets that both Andy and Svein-Arne arranged was in Byrkjelo, a small town in Norway's secluded fjord country. The only way to get there was by a small seaplane, so the trip required a flight that took us over snow-covered peaks before landing in a large fjord. We were cramped together like sardines while the plane maneuvered over the rough terrain, barely clearing the trees below. Upon hearing about the perilous flight required to make the trip, Mary Slaney almost canceled. The same was true of our sprinters. They were so scared during the flight that they almost passed out. In the end, the meet attracted hundreds of local people, and everyone was happy to have had a chance to be in such a spectacular, isolated place. The slopes of the snowcapped mountains that surrounded the track were the home of modern mink farms. Byrkjelo is still my favorite small-town meet. The organizers even arranged helicopter rides for athletes, most of whom took advantage of the once-in-a-lifetime experience. Most had never been in a helicopter before. The craft lifted the bug-eyed athletes straight up for one hundred meters, after which it made several turns around a lake before descending to the grass field. After that ride, I was hoping that they would forget about the next day's return flight to Oslo. Evidently, they didn't. Coming in for landing was no fun, but the prospect of clearing those trees again on takeoff served to reawaken their fears. The seaplane had to taxi at full throttle, hoping to gather enough speed to avoid the trees. Mary and athletes were not confident. After takeoff, our seaplane gathered speed and proceeded to fly toward the mountain range. The next thirty minutes were the most harrowing. As we started to slow and saw the approaching hillside full of trees, everyone froze in their seats. The pilot remained cool while nonchalantly glancing at us through the rearview mirror. We made it, as everyone knew we would, but after landing in a fjord, we found ourselves stranded by a roadside. Our instructions were to wait for a bus that would hopefully appear soon. The weather had turned cold with a stinging wind that made us shiver. Our athletes were tested to see if they were meant for the challenges of European travel, with the experienced athletes taking on the task of admonishing the complainers. In the end, few complained, and most even expressed a desire to return to the meet next year. Nobody made big fees, but it was a memorable trip. Those were the fun years. Whenever any manager wanted to get an invitation for an athlete who had been in Europe too long and was fading fast, Andy's favorite reply was, "Let's just say that the gentleman has outlived his usefulness and should go home." We doubted that Andy ever got more than three or four hours of sleep, since he was always traveling, arranging other meets, representing IAAF (International Amateur Athletic Federation), etc. Unfortunately, his health suffered from the stress, and he passed away years after we had retired from the European scene. Svein-Arne is no longer the meet organizer, but has taken over the job as Europe's track and field director and is involved with IAAF. And I'm sure he still has a million dollars' worth of stamps in his briefcase.

36. Pete's athletes waiting for a bus after a tense flight from Byrkjelo, Norway. Mary Decker Slaney, happy to be on the ground, is second from the left.

FREDDY SCHAFER, GERMANY

The Koblenz meeting, organized by Freddy Schafer, was one of the pleasant surprises on our summer schedule. Freddy, a semiretired postal director, and I formed a friendship that resulted in the guarantee that my athletes would have reliable opportunities to compete on a regular basis. Freddy and his friend, Karl Pretzer, pooled enough funds to start a meet. With Andy and Svein-Arne's help, Freddie was able to attract the best athletes from Eastern Europe, many of whom were content just to be able to compete outside of their home countries. I met some Latvian athletes and coaches, which gave me an opportunity to converse in our native language. Freddy made sure the top German athletes would be invited as well. During the first few years, he didn't have access to big purses or first-class accommodations. But he was nevertheless clever enough to convince athletes to come to Koblenz. His nickname became "Freddie the Fox" for his creative ways of making athletes happy. Hoping that the athletes would forget about the lack of luxury accommodations and small purses, he arranged delicious, all-you-can-eat after-meet dinners that were served in the basement of a friend's tavern. Each year the meet improved, and as the word spread, the small stadium was filled to capacity. Athletes were comfortably housed in the first-class hotels overlooking the Rhine River. Edwin Moses set a new world record in the 400-meter hurdles, Steve Ovett did the same in the 1,500 meters, and all of my mile to 1,500-meter runners improved their times. Freddy realized that inviting the best German athletes would also guarantee coverage on German television, resulting in more income for the following year's meets. We all enjoyed the warm atmosphere of the meet, the scenic Rheine region, and the historic city of Koblenz. Tom and I enjoyed our runs along the Rhine River, where we were able to watch the procession of boats and barges. Freddy was a resourceful promoter. After noticing a large gap in the summer schedule, he decided to quickly organize a meet and invite the world's best 110-meter hurdlers. His attitude was that athletes had to be somewhere in Europe, so it might as well be in Koblenz. The following year, they all showed up because Freddy had treated them so well the year before. With Eurovision and SKY networks broadcasting his meet, he didn't have to dish out the big bucks. "Freddy the Fox" knew what he was doing all along, and Koblenz became a not-to-be-missed meet. Freddie has visited us in Agoura, we have enjoyed treating him to a steak dinner when he is in town. We still keep in touch, hoping that he'll return again, this time for delicious ribs!

Joyce and I talk about one day returning to Europe to reacquaint ourselves with our friends who treated us so well.

THE EMERGENCE OF
PROFESSIONAL MANAGERS

Our sport has experienced a drastic change from the early 1980s to the present. Tom Jennings of Pacific Coast Club was the trailblazer who first arranged meets in Europe for his select athletes in the mid-1970s. There were no rules or guidelines set by the meet organizers. Money was usually paid under the table, often in foreign currencies that had to be exchanged each time athletes traveled to another country. Tom was a master when it came to making deals. He made creative side bets: if his jumper could clear eighteen feet, then he would receive a handsome payday. If he missed, the organizer wouldn't have to pay anything. Other times he agreed to a lump sum payment for his group. At a small meet in Finland, he made an agreement that, if the attendance was over three thousand spectators, he would receive a bonus. Tom paid close attention to the ticket counter and made frequent inquiries regarding the attendance figures. The last count he was given totaled 2,997, so Tom said, "I'll buy the last three tickets." The meet director quickly replied, "The ticket counter is closed." Both Tom and the meeting directors enjoyed the challenge of making such unusual arrangements. Meanwhile, our Federation and the IRS knew nothing of US athletes getting paid. In order to bring money home, athletes stuffed one-hundred-dollar bills in their pockets or hid them in their laundry. Others went as far as wearing special money vests around their stomachs. Upon arrival in the United States, they made sure they wore US Olympic team jackets so inspectors would give them a quick pass through the lines.

Slowly, other managers appeared on the circuit. Tony Campbell was the next in line, with Joe Douglas of Santa Monica Track Club and me following at about the same time. Our group of manager-agents was a diverse collection of former athletes, lawyers, educators, and coaches from many countries. One such manager was a former KGB agent from Russia and two (Michael Johnson and Renaldo Nehemiah) were former world-record holders. Early accommodations were sparse, and the food was ordinary at best. Most of our travel was on trains. Often I would arrive at a station to see Tony's and Joe's athletes stretched out on benches, trying to get some sleep. Again, it was Tom Jennings who came up with the idea of putting pressure on the organizers by publishing a managers' report card, listing each meet's score on hotels, food, travel assistance, and communication. This resulted in slow but noticeable changes. Meet organizers started to brag about their meet scores. Others followed, and today all Grand Prix—Golden Gala meets have top hotels, great food, and convenient air transportation. Not to be outdone, the organizers responded with a ranking of the managers, putting pressure on those who they thought should not be permitted to manage athletes.

The Zurich meetings in the late 1980s were the first to have managers sign contracts, listing the agreed sums with taxes taken out but leaving it up to the athletes to report finances to the IRS. The big shocker came when the British government imposed a 30 percent tax that was deducted from the athlete's total income. Big-time managers charged another 25 percent, so the athletes' income shrunk considerably. There were no more free rides, unless one chose not to report earnings that were not taxed.

Since Nike provided our transportation, Tom and I differed from other managers, since we only expected our athletes to cover phone costs and incidental expenses. Often I wanted to quit when some of my fellow managers started to steal athletes, cornering them in hotel lobbies, telling lies about me, using the "race card," and putting me in unfavorable situations.

After nearly twenty years, I decided that I had "made my contribution to the sport," the words Andy Norman aptly used when it was time for an athlete to fold up the tent in Europe and go home. It had become more of a frustrating exercise in survival than a fulfilling hobby. I learned that many people involved in the high-stakes game of international athletics were less than ethical. Even some of my athletes could not be trusted. For example, I received a call from a Spanish friend who wanted my 400-meter runner to appear in his meet. He suggested that I pay for the runner's travel expenses, for which the athlete would reimburse me after he collected his fee. My runner failed to tell me that he was injured. He scratched from the event and flew home without informing me. It was the last time I ever saw him. It was a hard lesson for me, and a sign that our sport was changing—and not for the better.

Another problem was that there were no rules or regulations with regards to the behavior of managers, especially when it involved the recruiting of other manager's athletes. Incidents of "athlete poaching" resulted in signed contracts between athlete and manager. The contracts were largely ignored, and unless I worked to establish a strong working relationship with my athlete, I faced the constant risk of having them leave my group. Tom and I often heard remarks by some managers that ridiculed us because of our age, calling us the "old farts."

They said that we were "out of touch" and could no longer be viewed as effective bargainers. Nike assigned me to help arrange competitions for their newer athletes, which went well for the first year. After the young athletes had established good marks during the first year, they were offered bigger fees by other managers and poached from my group. I lost some athletes, but it was heartening that most stayed with me. A number wanted to come back to my group when they realized the promises of their new manager were overblown. And so it went.

I missed my family and friends when they could not be with me. Travel to formerly exotic places had lost its appeal. I no longer found the patience to endure the long waits in airports or the hassles of dealing with lost luggage. Travel arrangements to hotels and meets continued to be a headache. We were also getting tired of standing in lines in hotel lobbies waiting for the athletes' payment. Some summers I came home for a week or two, only to return a short time later for the August and early September meets in Zurich, Cologne, Monaco, and Berlin. It became increasingly difficult to adjust to the jet lag caused by shuttling between nine different time zones. Once home, I wished I had a whole month to recoup my energies and get ready for school.

Despite the inconveniences, I would not have traded my involvement with athletes and meet organizers. I had the privilege of attending four Olympic Games and have established lifelong friendships. I was able to travel to twenty-five different countries and participate in track competitions in eighty-three different cities. I always had the companionship of my athletes, and at times, my family, which provided me with so many rich and unforgettable experiences. Yes—"wonderful memories are made of this."

IN MEMORY

All of us who knew Tom Sturak were saddened by his gradual physical and mental decline caused by Alzheimer's disease. I remember visiting him in his "eagle-nest" home above Topanga Canyon. We discussed our best memories with meet organizers (Svein-Arne Hansen telling the rabbit to be sure to take pictures of Oslo, since he would never be invited again, Wilfried's memory of sharing a Rothschild wine in Prague, dinners in elegant restaurants with Mark Mastalir and Mark Bossardet, Reebok's directors who toured Europe with us.) Sadly, these wonderful memories gradually faded from his consciousness. He usually read late into the night. I would ask him about the latest book he had read, but he usually had no memory of it. Tom passed away on April 29, 2011. Jacqueline organized a memorable day of celebration that attracted many of Tom's friends, all sharing their best moments with him. It was a fitting tribute to such a unique individual.

We also miss Mike Larrabee, a former Trojan and the Tokyo 400-meter Olympic champion. He fought a courageous battle with pancreatic cancer, in which he was able to prolong his life for nearly four years after the doctors had given him only months to live. With his best friend, John Bragg, by his side, he climbed mountains, went on strenuous hikes, and challenged the ski slopes. He always maintained a positive attitude toward life, never acknowledging the concept of quitting and continuing to engage in innocent acts of "terrorizing" with John. All of us loved watching Mike compete. With his head bobbing from side to side, he was instantly recognized in a field of 400-meter runners. The bobbing head usually had a sly grin on its face as he passed the rest of the runners down the homestretch. The excitement he brought to a one-lap race was unique; USC track has never been quite the same since he left.

We also miss John Pennel, a colorful all-around athlete from the Bayou country. He always put his family first and was a fabulous role model for his children. He was a four-time world-record holder in the pole vault and recipient of the Sullivan Award for the year's outstanding amateur athlete. He had a wonderful

37. Great friends John & Mary Bragg and Margaret Larrabee, Ajijic, Mexico, 2008.

sense of humor, and his presence always guaranteed continuous laughter. He and Carolyn loved being with friends, often inviting fellow athletes and coaches to his home and entertaining us with his singing and guitar renditions of popular songs. When John, Mike Larrabee, Bill Toomey, and Ron Whitney got together at Lake Tahoe, their serious training for the Olympic trials was always accompanied (and often interrupted) by jokes, laughter, and imitations of comedians.

LIFE IN SEMI-RETIREMENT

Life has been good to us. We no longer play the gypsy role traveling the world, we have settled down in Agoura, CA with its small-town charm and year-around sunshine. If the heat gets to be too intense, we are a short drive from Malibu, where we can enjoy the refreshing ocean breezes. We also drive up to Carmel-by-the-Sea a couple times a year where we have a second home that is a vacation rental, we enjoy it whenever there is not a renter! We take long walks and I enjoy taking photos of the scenic area, including the unique homes, the surfers and the beauty of the Monterey Bay area.

THE PETERSONS FAMILY IN 2015

COREY, our youngest daughter, and her family have settled down with us in Agoura recently, after spending 15 years on the beautiful Laurel Springs Ranch in the mountains above Santa Barbara. Ever since her elementary school days, Corey has always loved horses. Whenever we stopped by a pasture, she could coax a horse to walk up to her so she could stroke its nose. The horses recognized Corey as a person who could be trusted, our own horse-whisperer. She spent hours at equestrian events, and loved learning dressage and cross-country riding in her younger years. She has become proficient in using equine educational treatment with horses to help people who suffer from stress and addiction. Corey met her husband Kabir while spending three years in an Ashram in India. Kabir has become a professional photographer and is a master paraglider. While living in Santa Barbara, whenever Corey had time, and the warm updrafts off of the mountain ridges were suitable, she joined Kabir for flights over the city and surrounding countryside. Their two children Talulah (10) and Mateo (8) attended Waldorf School in Santa Barbara, which provided a rich and unusual educational environment, stressing a natural progression of lifelong learning skills in a peaceful environment. Their family now lives temporarily with us. The arrangement has been very practical for them, since Corey is able to work with her horse equine treatments in nearby Malibu, and Kabir is able to work as a manager for Acro-Yoga Company from home. In spare time, he is a volunteer first responder for the Santa Barbara Fire Department.

38. Talulah, Mateo and Corey, 2014

MARNI, our oldest daughter, her son Tyler (22), and daughter Morgan (21) are living adult lives now. Marni raised her kids here in the Agoura area, also spending 5 years in Hawaii and 5 years in Florida. In 2008 they moved back to California and lived with Joyce and me. They were more than happy to return to California to be around our family for love and support. Joyce and I are very proud the way Marni has dedicated herself to her children as a single mom.

39. Morgan, Tyler and Marni, 2014

Morgan was a 4 year member and captain her senior year of Agoura High School's National Championship cheerleading team, with Marni acting as the team assistant. Morgan has blossomed into a confident and adventurous young lady, having graduated from Moorpark Community College with classes in psychology, speech, nutrition and physical fitness, resulting in a Personal Training Certification. She also enjoyed classes in the dance program. We love how she applies her knowledge by combining an active lifestyle and a healthy diet, along with being so positive and motivating. Along with her boyfriend Spencer, they have been living on Oahu's North Shore for 9 months now and are traveling the Orient as this book goes to print. The two of them have a long bucket list. This is only the beginning of their travels and adventures. It's not the destination, it's the journey! Seeing her so happy, we share in her enthusiasm for life.

Tyler has lived in San Clemente for 2 ½ years with his girlfriend Jessy, whom he met when they lived in Florida, and their dog Kona. Jessy moved out to California to go to college at FIDM. Tyler has completed his studies in business management at Saddleback Community College and is now happy working in San Clemente for a software company. Tyler first learned to surf at the age of 4 on the North Shore in Hawaii and has developed into an accomplished competitive surfer. He and Jessy love living a couple blocks from the beach where they enjoy surfing together daily.

Joyce and I are proud of the way Marni has dedicated herself to helping both Morgan and Tyler in becoming such fine young people. She will always be an amazing mother, but can now also focus on her own life and use her skills as a creative organizer and planner while troubleshooting for executive accounting clients. She is happily in a relationship with a wonderful man, we are so happy for her!

Words cannot express how proud we are of our two girls. They have enriched our lives and continue to impress in the way they are raising their children.

40. The Petersons family, 2014. Top from left; Kabir, Tyler, Marni and Morgan. Bottom from left; Mateo, Corey, Talulah, Joyce and Pete.

ACKNOWLEDGEMENTS

I am fortunate to have the support of my good friends and family in the writing of *Run for Fun*. They all have my deepest gratitude. Dick Weeks, a former runner and longtime friend, provided invaluable support in the compilation, formatting, and editing of the first edit of my memoir. We spent countless hours reviewing drafts, organizing material, and negotiating the daunting challenges of the publishing process. Thankfully, Dick had previously published his own travel memoir on birds, so his familiarity with the process was invaluable.

Special thanks to former runners, colleagues, and longtime friends Jim Bush, Ron Whitney, Martin Levine, Mike Manley, Dick Weeks, Bill Scobey, Tom Petranoff, Marty Liquori and Harry Marra for contributing their fond memories of our times together.

My wife, Joyce, an English teacher, patiently read and reread chapters and was a much-appreciated source of valuable feedback in both edits of this book along with her memories of our time in Saudi Arabia.

My daughters, Marni and Corey, for their continued support of me writing my memoir. Marni took on the second edit of this book with passion and love, committing endless hours to make sure it was complete and accurate.